JANE KENDEIGH

Brave Nurse of WORLD WAR II

by Emma Carlson Berne   illustrated by Karen De La Vega

CAPSTONE PRESS
a capstone imprint

Published by Capstone Press, an imprint of Capstone
1710 Roe Crest Drive, North Mankato, Minnesota 56003
capstonepub.com

Library of Congress Cataloging-in-Publication Data
Names: Berne, Emma Carlson, 1979– author. | Vega, Karen de la, illustrator.
Title: Jane Kendeigh : brave nurse of World War II / by Emma Carlson Berne ; illustrations by Karen De La Vega.

Description: North Mankato, Minnesota : Capstone Press, [2024] | Series: Women warriors of World War II | Includes bibliographical references. | Audience: Ages 8–11 | Audience: Grades 4–6 | Summary: "An inspiring graphic novel about Jane Kendeigh, a nurse who helped wounded soldiers in combat zones during World War II. During World War II, the United States' fight against the Japanese on islands in the Pacific was intense and deadly. To help respond to casualties in battle, the U.S. Navy trained 122 nurses to aid wounded soldiers in combat zones. The first nurse to do so was Jane Kendeigh, a 22-year-old woman from Ohio. In March 1945, Kendeigh's first assignment was to help soldiers fighting in the Battle of Iwo Jima—a fierce battle with many casualties. With bravery and determination, she and other nurses helped thousands of soldiers in that battle—and many more in the Battle of Okinawa. In this full-color graphic novel, discover more about this courageous nurse who braved the battlefield to help U.S. soldiers"—Provided by publisher.
Identifiers: LCCN 2023002021 (print) | LCCN 2023002022 (ebook) | ISBN 9781669013549 (hardcover) | ISBN 9781669013495 (paperback) | ISBN 9781669013501 (pdf) | ISBN 9781669013525 (kindle edition) | ISBN 9781669013532 (epub)
Subjects: LCSH: Kendeigh, Jane, 1922–1987—Juvenile literature. | Aviation nursing—United States—History—20th century—Juvenile literature. | World War, 1939–1945—Medical care—Pacific Area—Juvenile literature. | Nurses—Biography—Juvenile literature. | World War, 1939–1945—Participation, Female—Juvenile literature. | United States—Armed Forces—Nurses—Biography—Juvenile literature. | Kendeigh, Jane, 1922–1987—Comic books, strips, etc. | Aviation nursing—United States—History—20th century—Comic books, strips, etc. | World War, 1939–1945—Medical care—Pacific Area—Comic books, strips, etc. | Nurses—Biography—Comic books, strips, etc. | World War, 1939–1945—Participation, Female—Comic books, strips, etc. | United States—Armed Forces—Nurses—Biography—Comic books, strips, etc.
Classification: LCC D807.U6 K463 2023 (print) | LCC D807.U6 (ebook) | DDC 940.54/7573 [B]—dc23/eng/20230214
LC record available at https://lccn.loc.gov/2023002021
LC ebook record available at https://lccn.loc.gov/2023002022

Editorial Credits
Editor: Ericka Smith; Designer: Sarah Bennett; Production Specialist: Katy LaVigne

All internet sites appearing in back matter were available and accurate when this book was sent to press.

Design Elements: Shutterstock/Here

Direct quotations appear in bold italicized text on the following pages:
Page 20, April 7, 2021, *Tara Ross* blog post, "This Day in History: The First Navy Flight Nurse," taraross.com

Printed and bound in the USA. 5425

TABLE OF CONTENTS

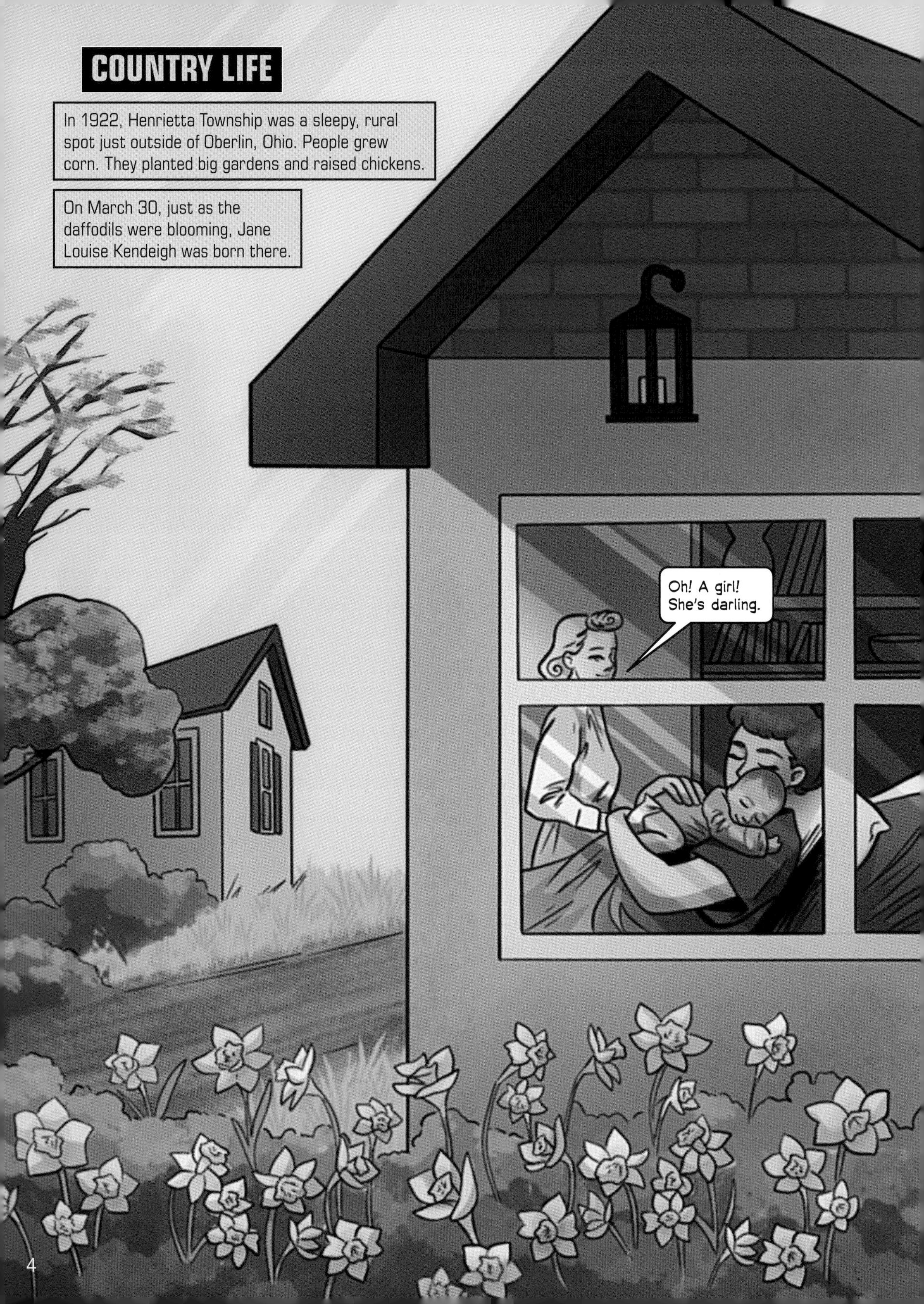
COUNTRY LIFE
In 1922, Henrietta Township was a sleepy, rural spot just outside of Oberlin, Ohio. People grew corn. They planted big gardens and raised chickens.
On March 30, just as the daffodils were blooming, Jane Louise Kendeigh was born there.
Oh! A girl! She's darling.

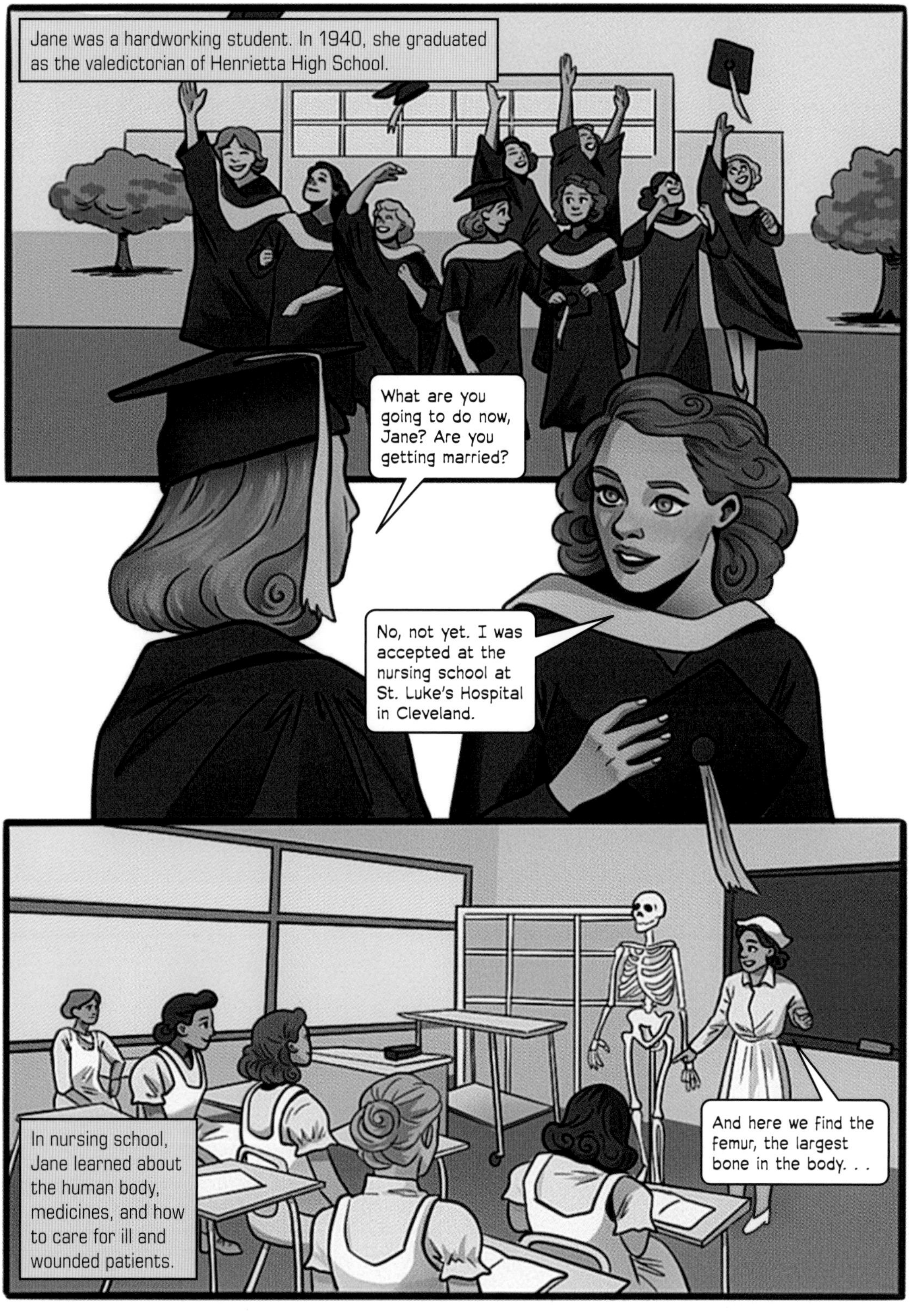

Jane was a hardworking student. In 1940, she graduated as the valedictorian of Henrietta High School.
What are you going to do now, Jane? Are you getting married?
No, not yet. I was accepted at the nursing school at St. Luke's Hospital in Cleveland.
In nursing school, Jane learned about the human body, medicines, and how to care for ill and wounded patients.
And here we find the femur, the largest bone in the body. . .

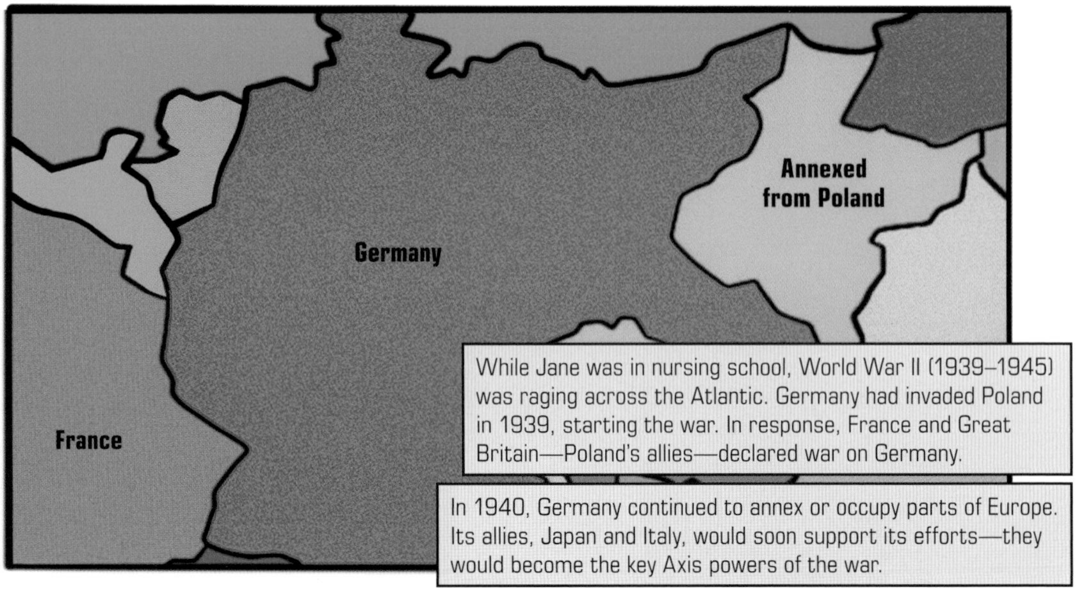
Annexed from Poland
Germany
France
While Jane was in nursing school, World War II (1939–1945) was raging across the Atlantic. Germany had invaded Poland in 1939, starting the war. In response, France and Great Britain—Poland's allies—declared war on Germany.
In 1940, Germany continued to annex or occupy parts of Europe. Its allies, Japan and Italy, would soon support its efforts—they would become the key Axis powers of the war.

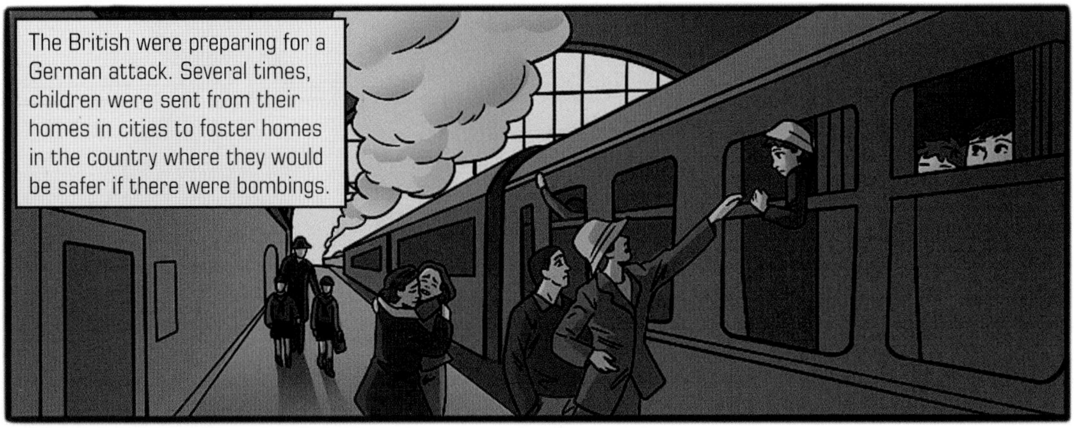
The British were preparing for a German attack. Several times, children were sent from their homes in cities to foster homes in the country where they would be safer if there were bombings.

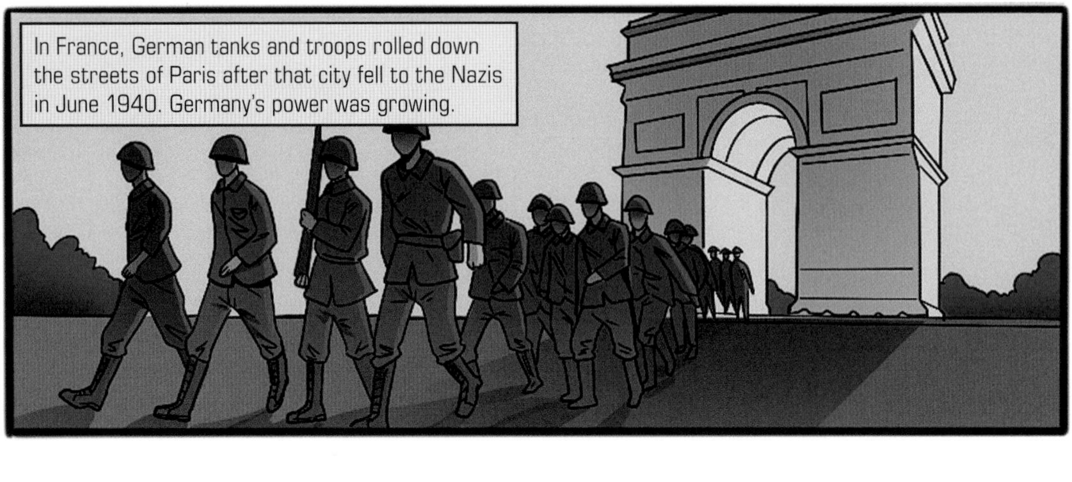
In France, German tanks and troops rolled down the streets of Paris after that city fell to the Nazis in June 1940. Germany's power was growing.

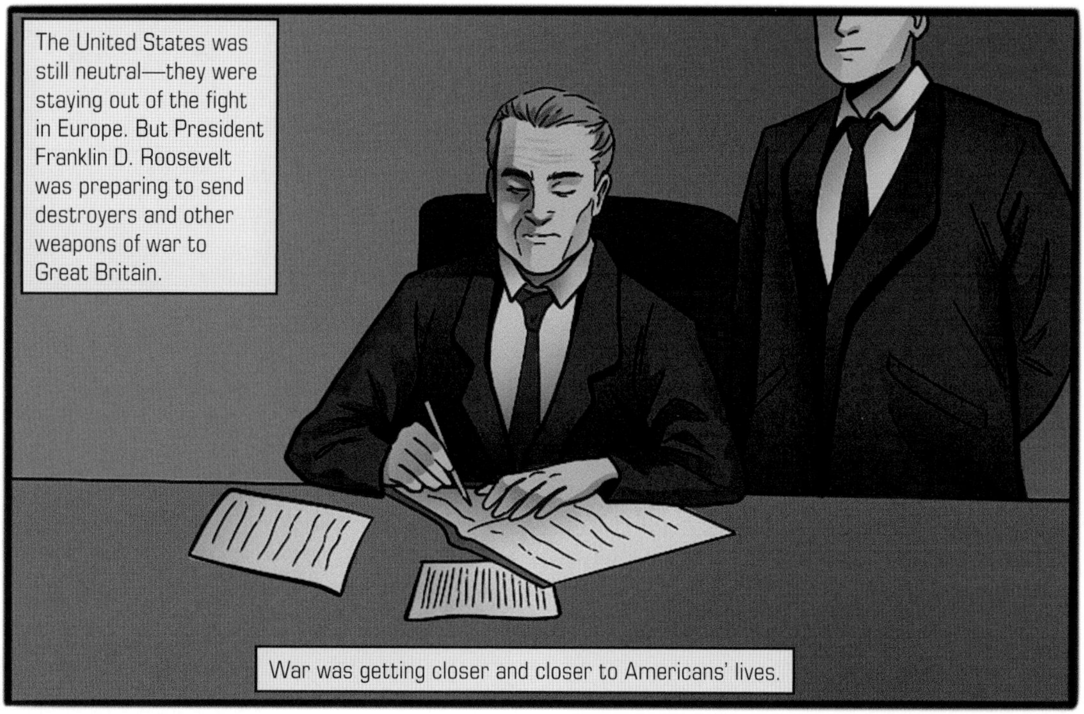
The United States was still neutral—they were staying out of the fight in Europe. But President Franklin D. Roosevelt was preparing to send destroyers and other weapons of war to Great Britain.
War was getting closer and closer to Americans' lives.

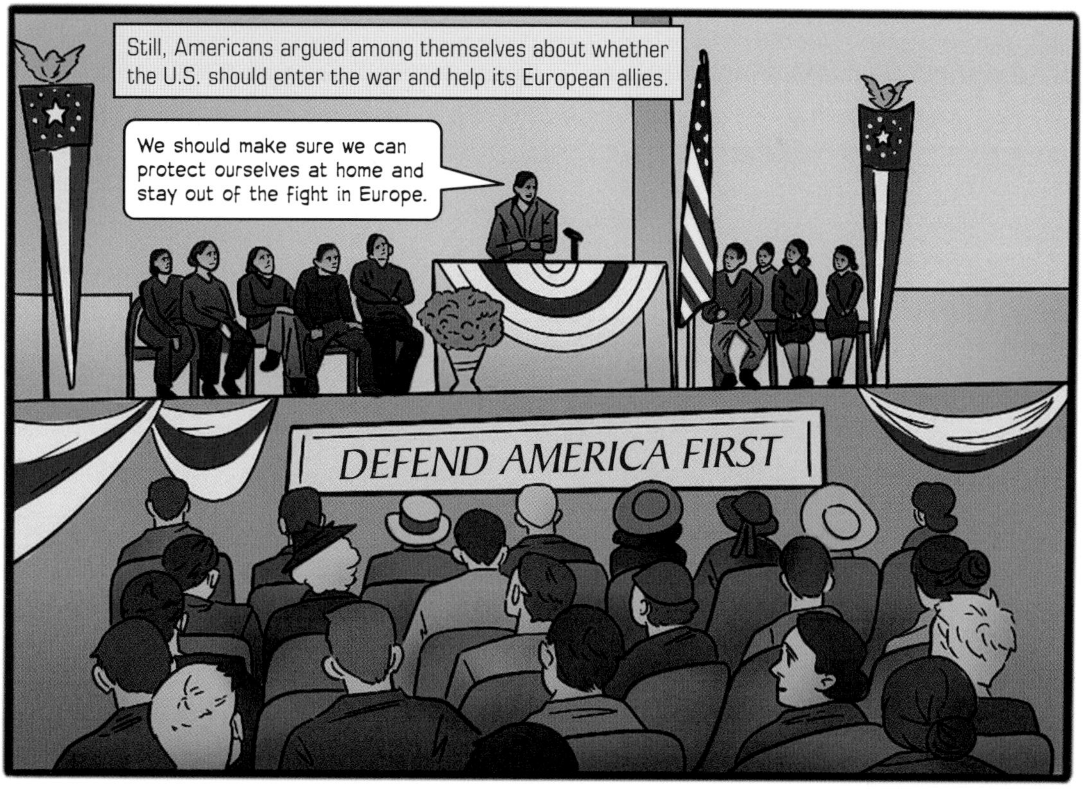
Still, Americans argued among themselves about whether the U.S. should enter the war and help its European allies.
We should make sure we can protect ourselves at home and stay out of the fight in Europe.
DEFEND AMERICA FIRST

PREPARING FOR WAR

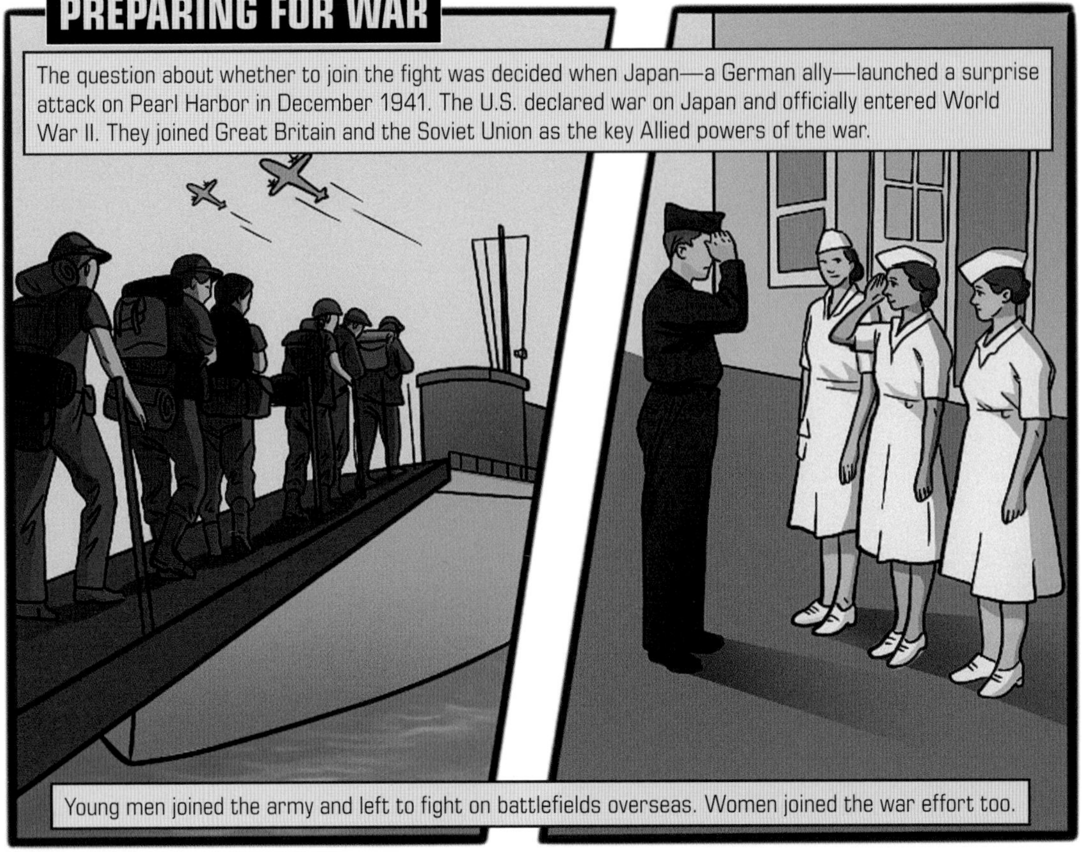
The question about whether to join the fight was decided when Japan—a German ally—launched a surprise attack on Pearl Harbor in December 1941. The U.S. declared war on Japan and officially entered World War II. They joined Great Britain and the Soviet Union as the key Allied powers of the war.
Young men joined the army and left to fight on battlefields overseas. Women joined the war effort too.

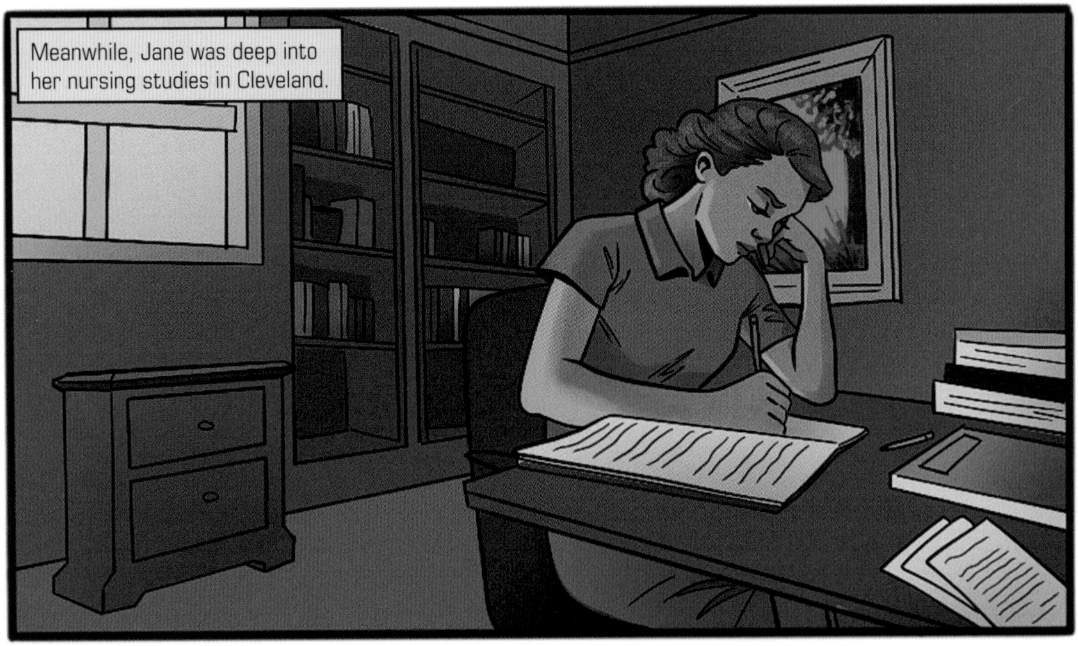
Meanwhile, Jane was deep into her nursing studies in Cleveland.

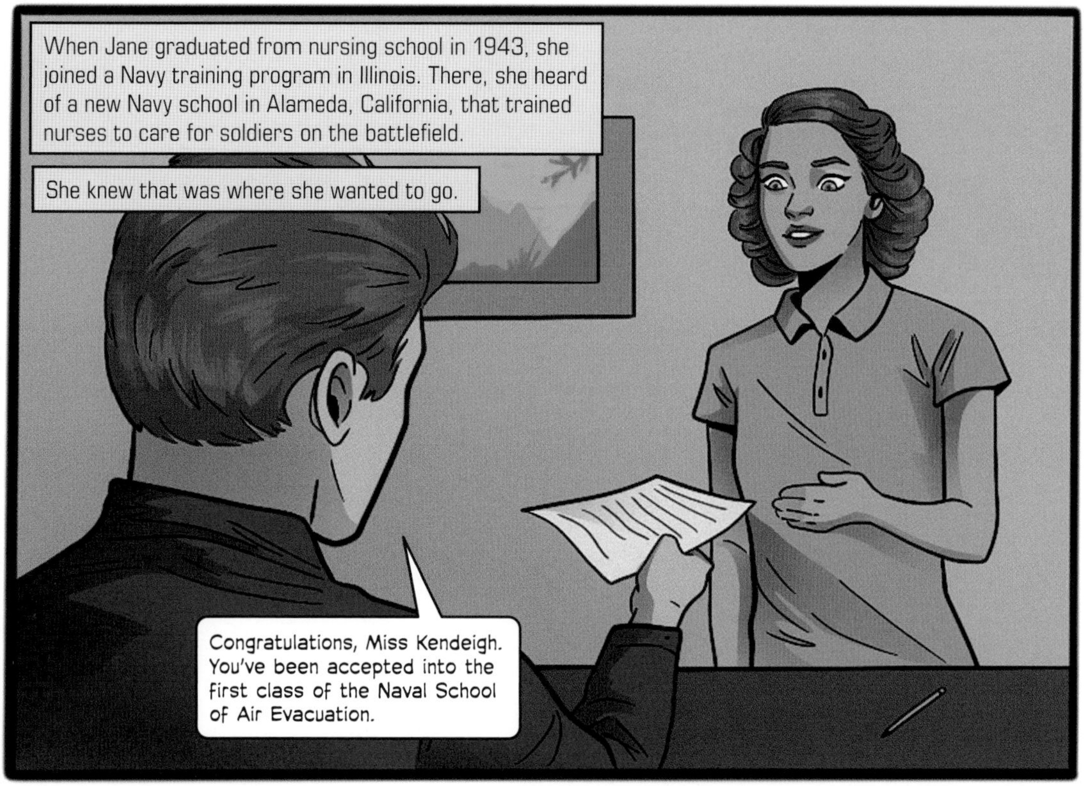
When Jane graduated from nursing school in 1943, she joined a Navy training program in Illinois. There, she heard of a new Navy school in Alameda, California, that trained nurses to care for soldiers on the battlefield.
She knew that was where she wanted to go.
Congratulations, Miss Kendeigh. You've been accepted into the first class of the Naval School of Air Evacuation.

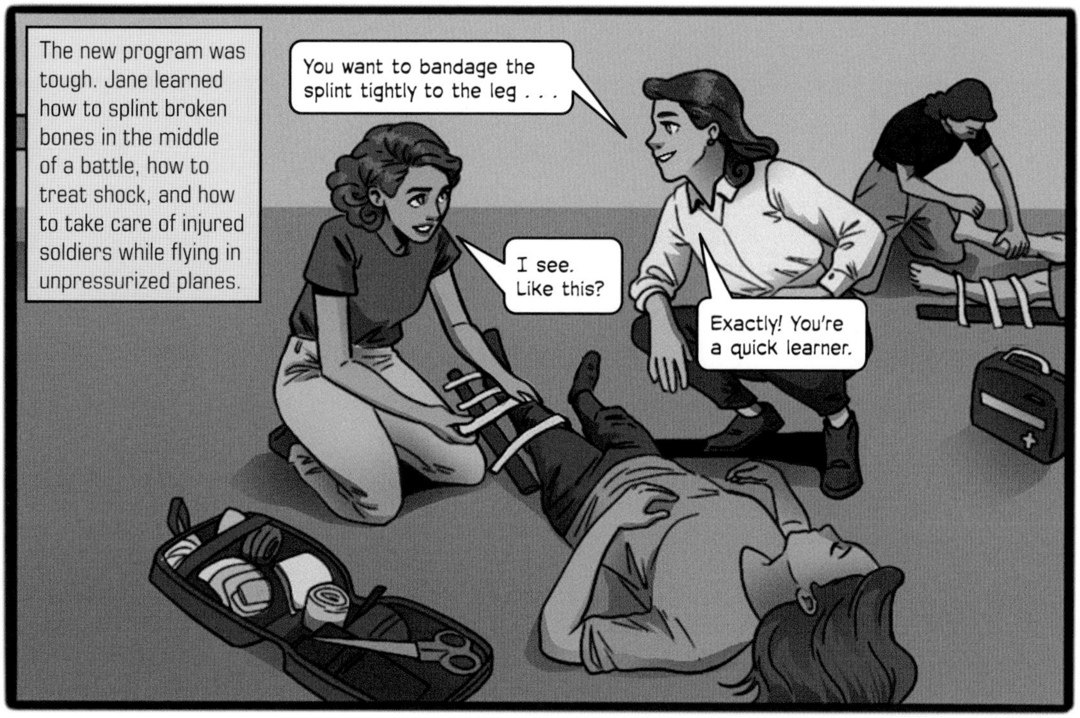
The new program was tough. Jane learned how to splint broken bones in the middle of a battle, how to treat shock, and how to take care of injured soldiers while flying in unpressurized planes.
You want to bandage the splint tightly to the leg . . .
I see. Like this?
Exactly! You're a quick learner.

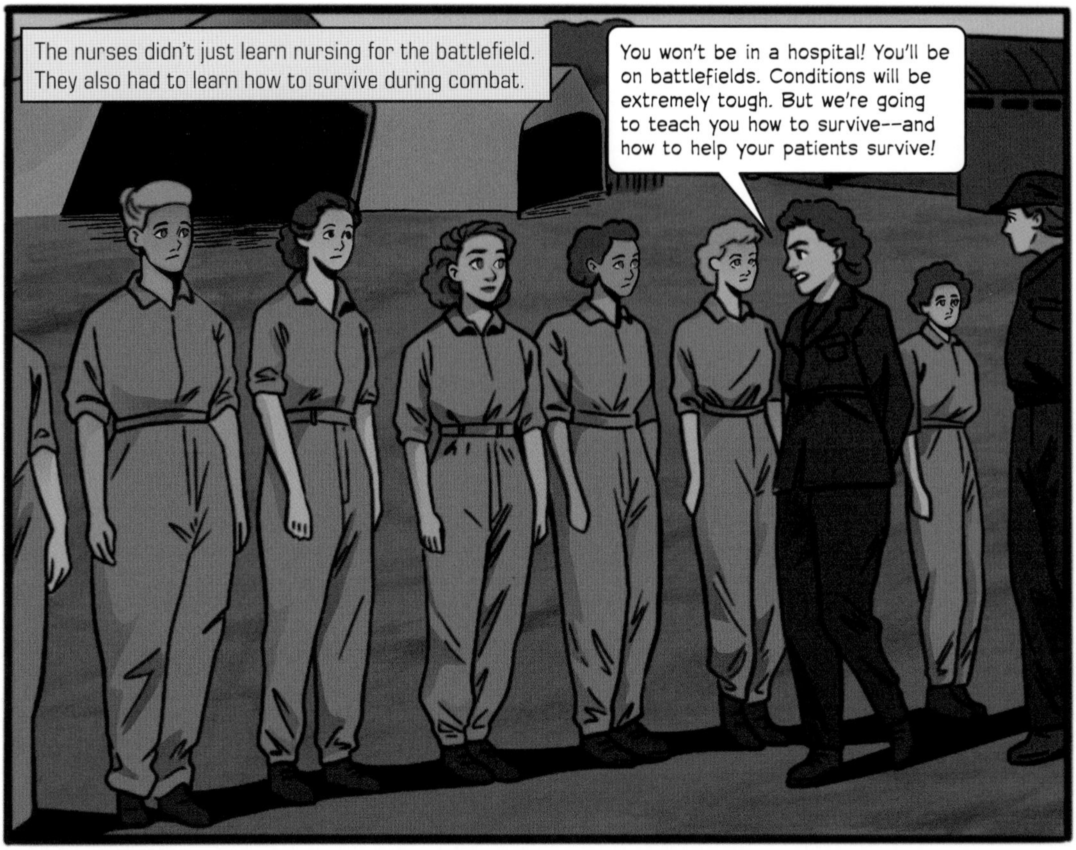
The nurses didn't just learn nursing for the battlefield. They also had to learn how to survive during combat.
You won't be in a hospital! You'll be on battlefields. Conditions will be extremely tough. But we're going to teach you how to survive--and how to help your patients survive!

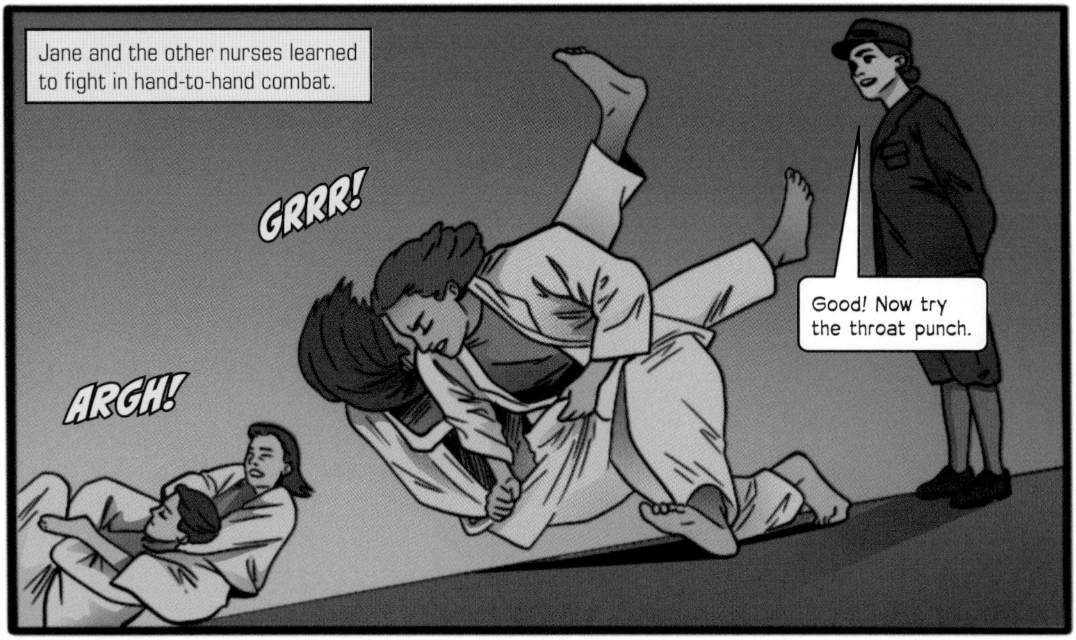
Jane and the other nurses learned to fight in hand-to-hand combat.
GRRR!
ARGH!
Good! Now try the throat punch.

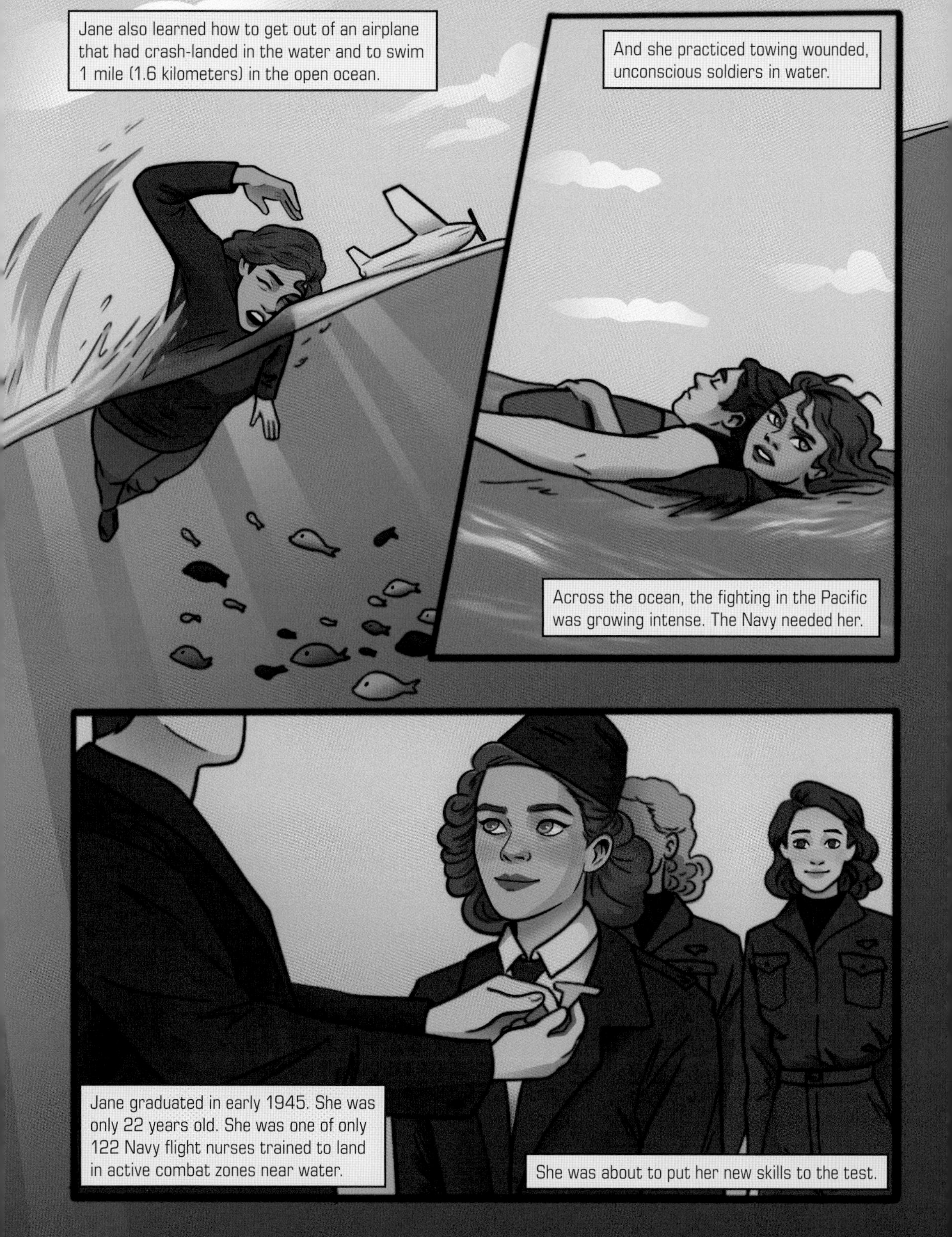
Jane also learned how to get out of an airplane that had crash-landed in the water and to swim 1 mile (1.6 kilometers) in the open ocean.
And she practiced towing wounded, unconscious soldiers in water.
Across the ocean, the fighting in the Pacific was growing intense. The Navy needed her.
Jane graduated in early 1945. She was only 22 years old. She was one of only 122 Navy flight nurses trained to land in active combat zones near water.
She was about to put her new skills to the test.

GOING TO IWO JIMA

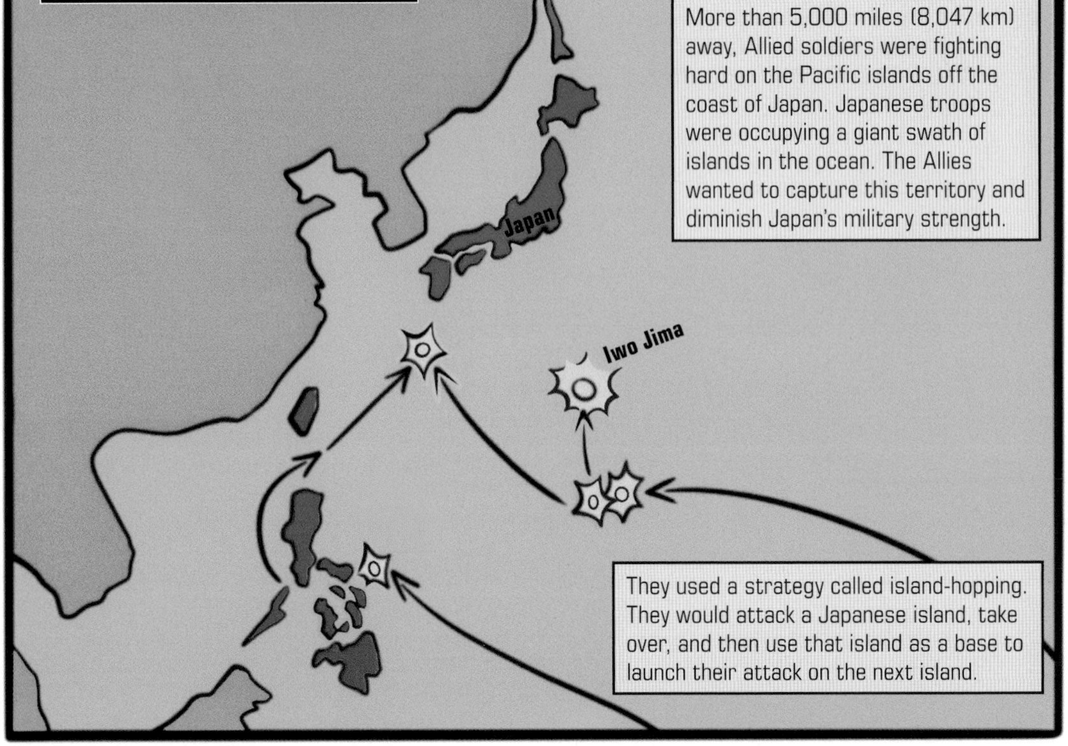
More than 5,000 miles (8,047 km) away, Allied soldiers were fighting hard on the Pacific islands off the coast of Japan. Japanese troops were occupying a giant swath of islands in the ocean. The Allies wanted to capture this territory and diminish Japan's military strength.
Japan
Iwo Jima
They used a strategy called island-hopping. They would attack a Japanese island, take over, and then use that island as a base to launch their attack on the next island.

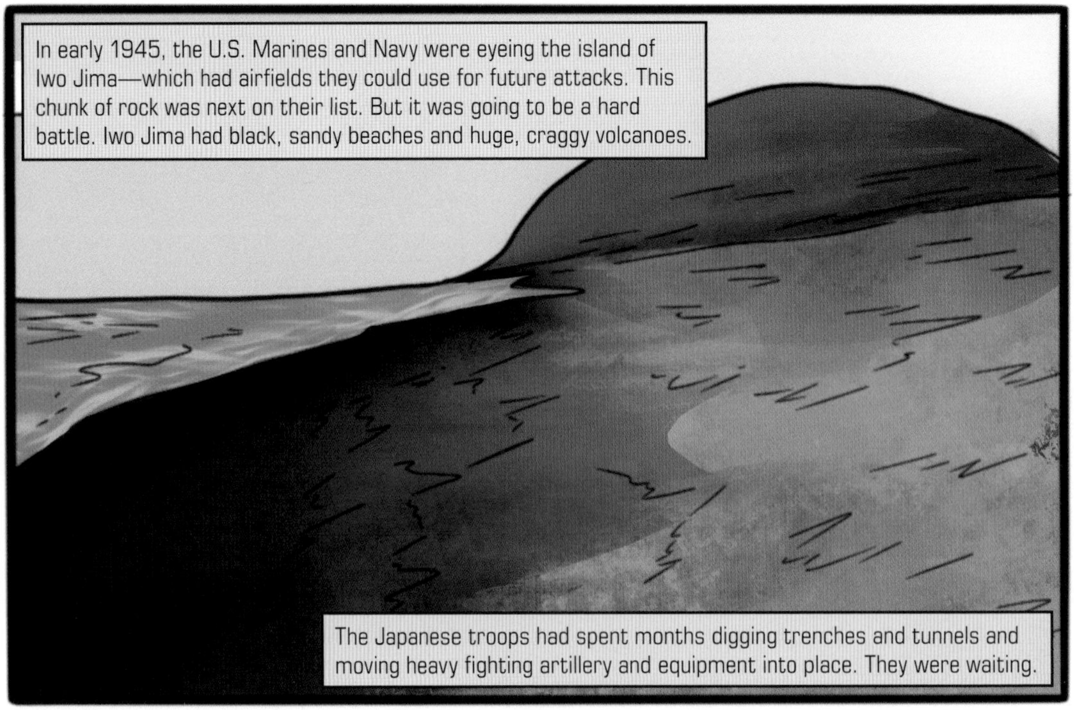
In early 1945, the U.S. Marines and Navy were eyeing the island of Iwo Jima—which had airfields they could use for future attacks. This chunk of rock was next on their list. But it was going to be a hard battle. Iwo Jima had black, sandy beaches and huge, craggy volcanoes.
The Japanese troops had spent months digging trenches and tunnels and moving heavy fighting artillery and equipment into place. They were waiting.

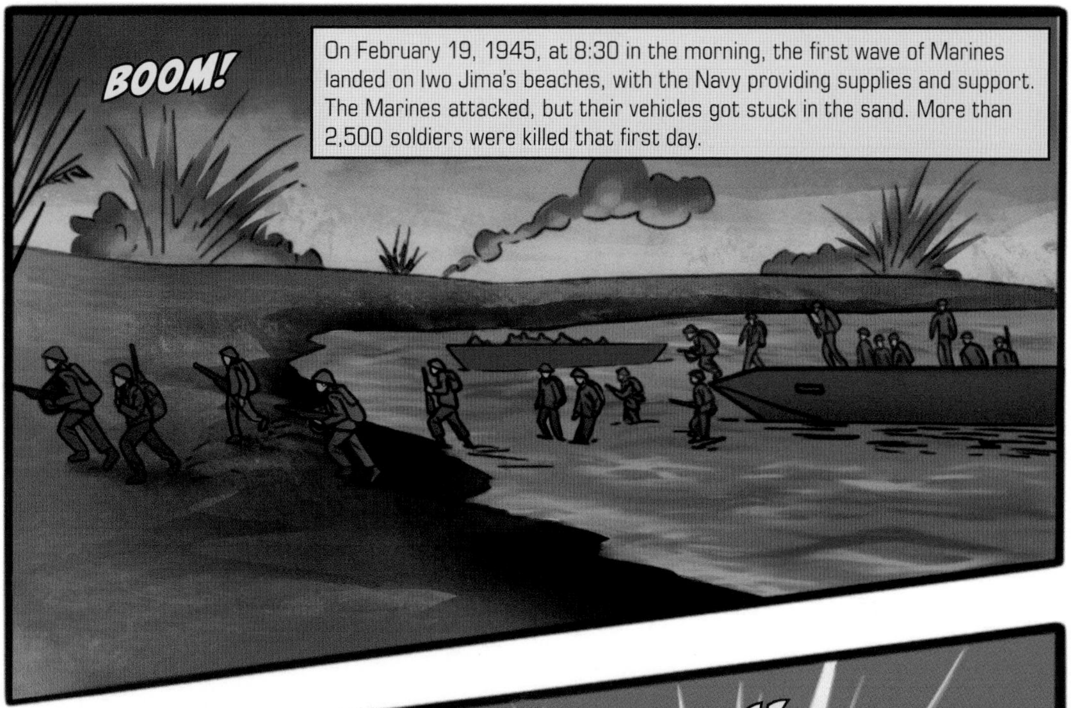
BOOM!
On February 19, 1945, at 8:30 in the morning, the first wave of Marines landed on Iwo Jima's beaches, with the Navy providing supplies and support. The Marines attacked, but their vehicles got stuck in the sand. More than 2,500 soldiers were killed that first day.

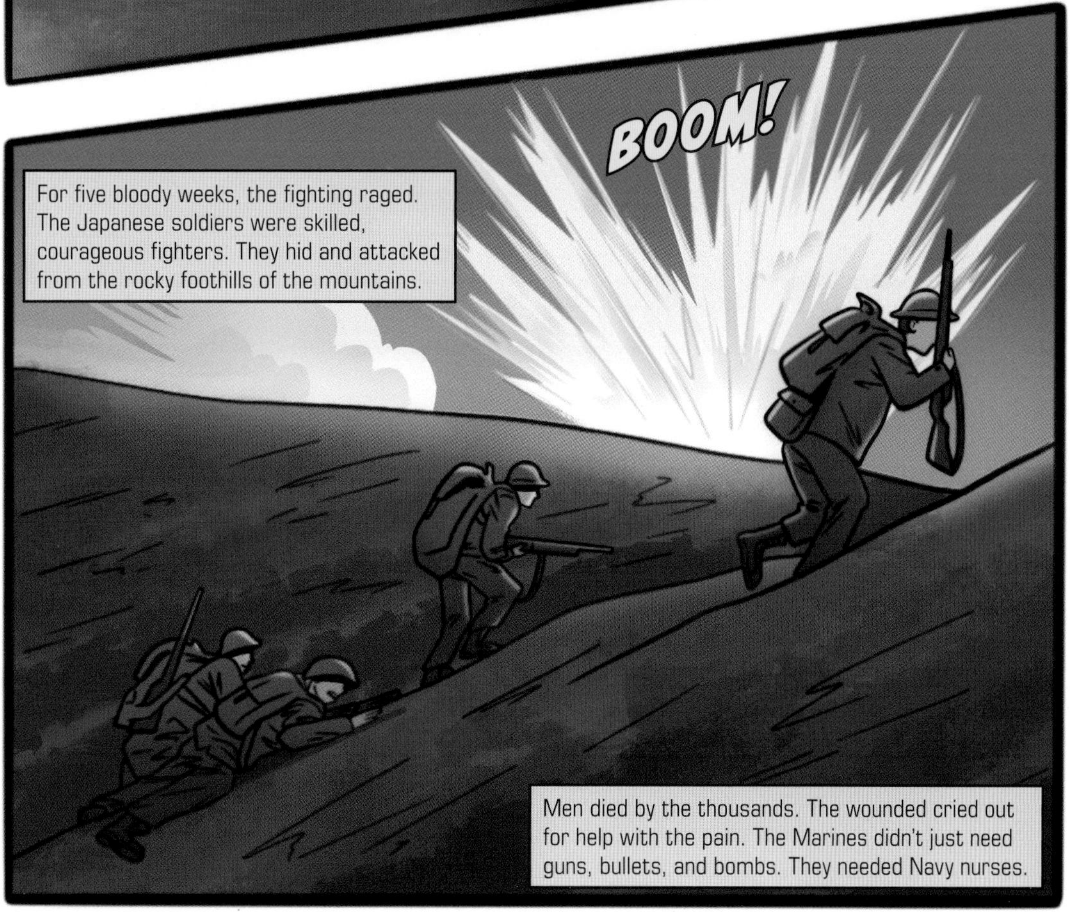
BOOM!
For five bloody weeks, the fighting raged. The Japanese soldiers were skilled, courageous fighters. They hid and attacked from the rocky foothills of the mountains.
Men died by the thousands. The wounded cried out for help with the pain. The Marines didn't just need guns, bullets, and bombs. They needed Navy nurses.

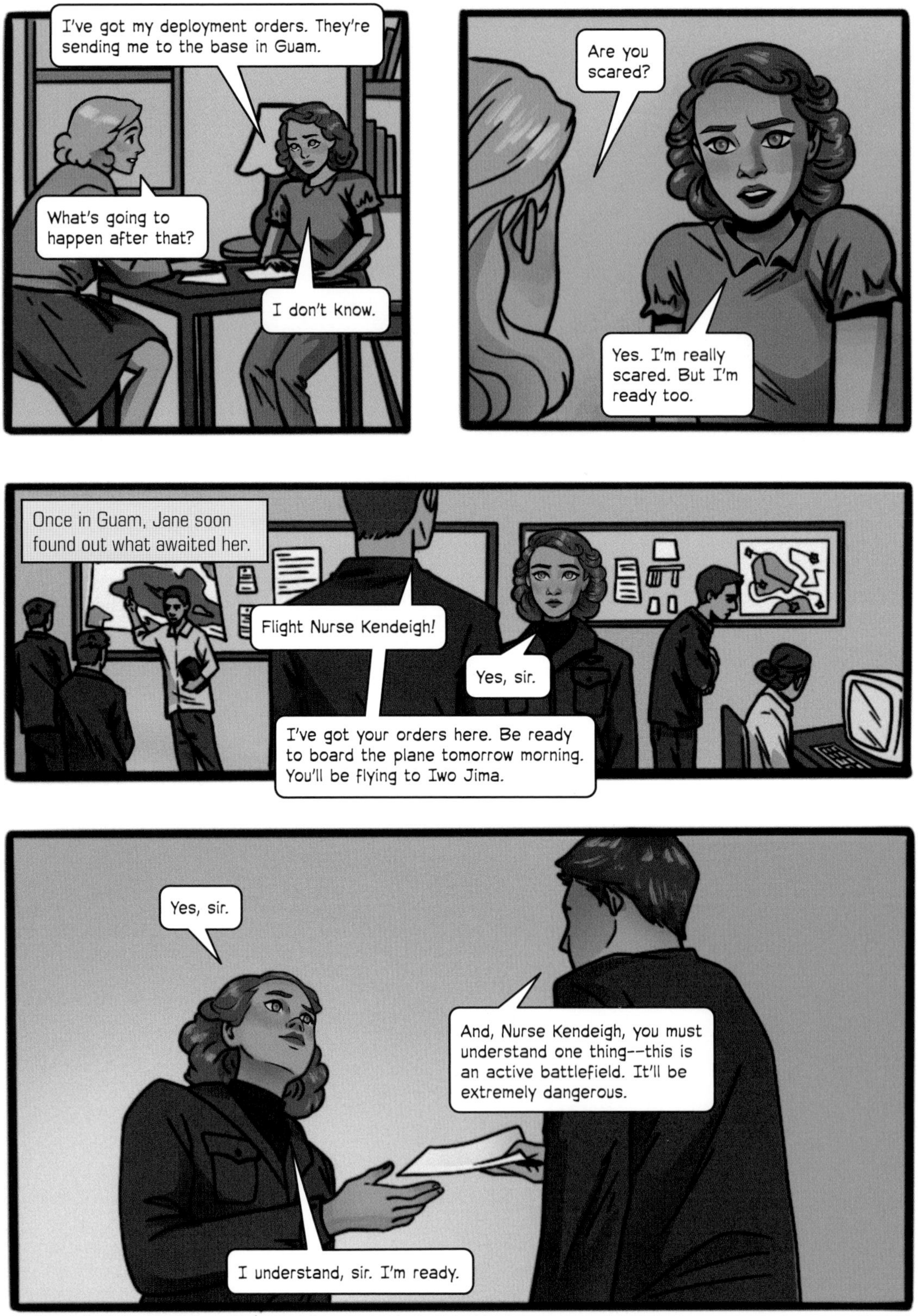
I've got my deployment orders. They're sending me to the base in Guam.
What's going to happen after that?
I don't know.
Are you scared?
Yes. I'm really scared. But I'm ready too.
Once in Guam, Jane soon found out what awaited her.
Flight Nurse Kendeigh!
Yes, sir.
I've got your orders here. Be ready to board the plane tomorrow morning. You'll be flying to Iwo Jima.
Yes, sir.
And, Nurse Kendeigh, you must understand one thing--this is an active battlefield. It'll be extremely dangerous.
I understand, sir. I'm ready.

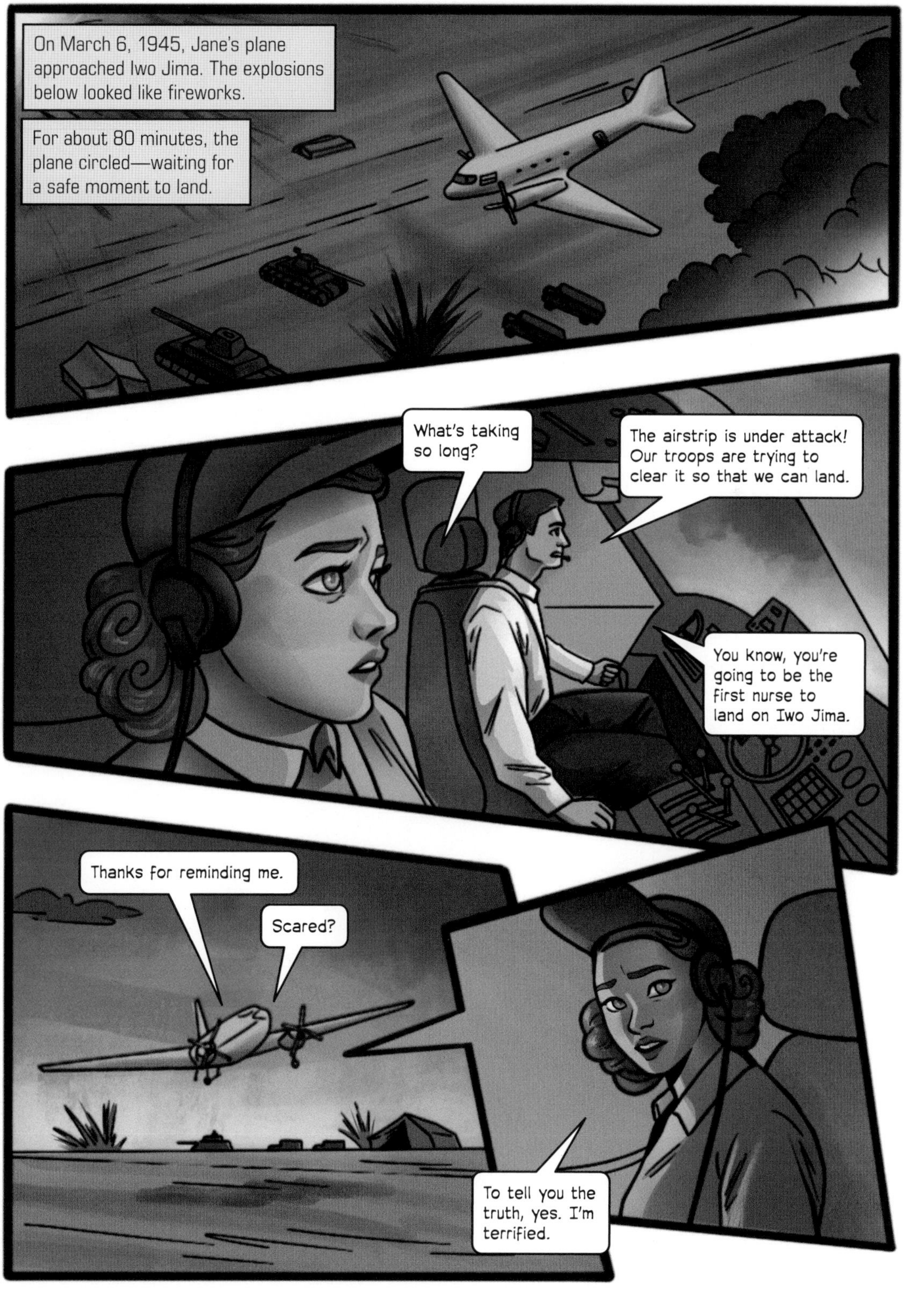

On March 6, 1945, Jane's plane approached Iwo Jima. The explosions below looked like fireworks.
For about 80 minutes, the plane circled—waiting for a safe moment to land.
What's taking so long?
The airstrip is under attack! Our troops are trying to clear it so that we can land.
You know, you're going to be the first nurse to land on Iwo Jima.
Thanks for reminding me.
Scared?
To tell you the truth, yes. I'm terrified.

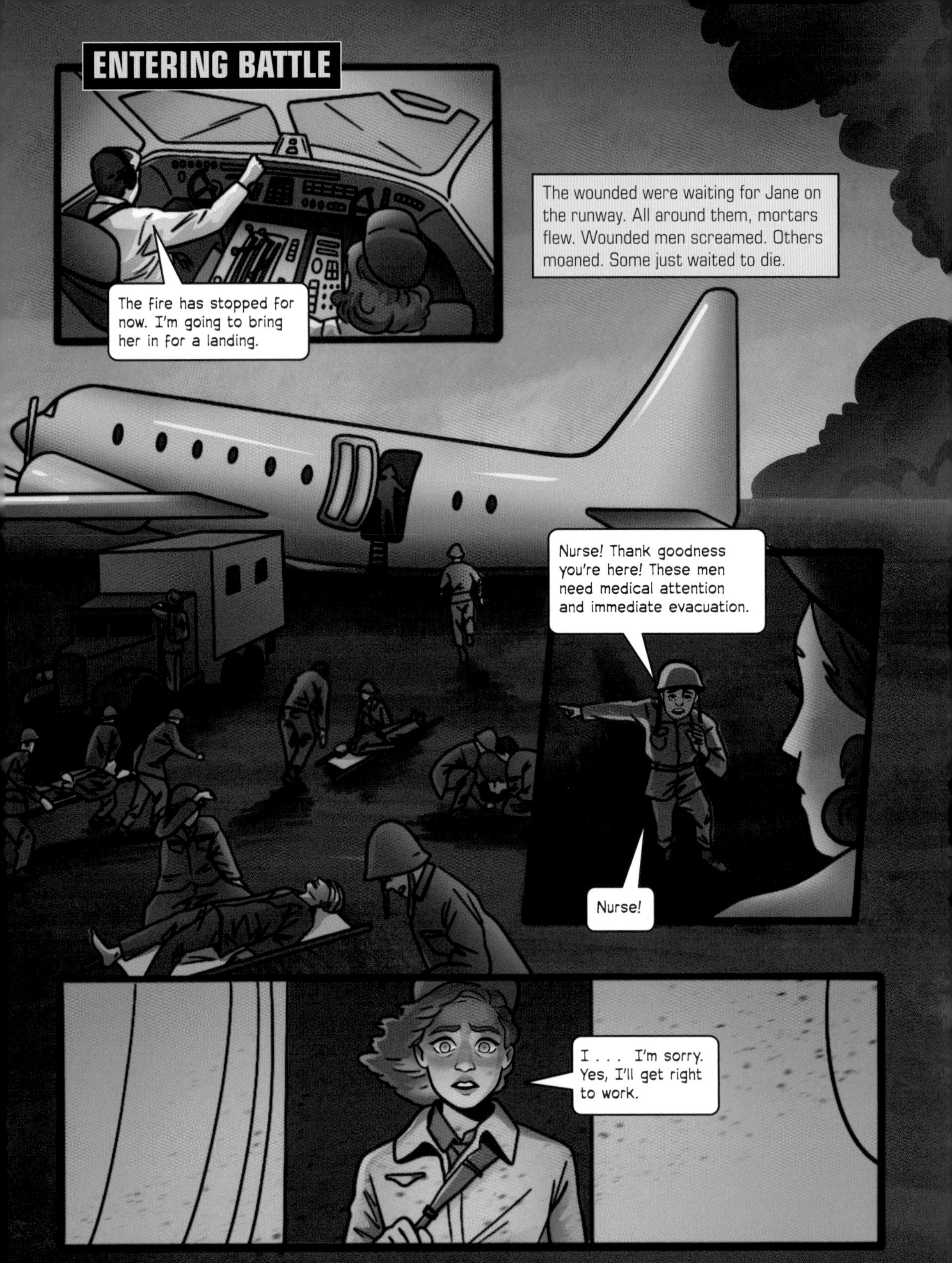
ENTERING BATTLE
The fire has stopped for now. I'm going to bring her in for a landing.
The wounded were waiting for Jane on the runway. All around them, mortars flew. Wounded men screamed. Others moaned. Some just waited to die.
Nurse! Thank goodness you're here! These men need medical attention and immediate evacuation.
Nurse!
I . . . I'm sorry. Yes, I'll get right to work.

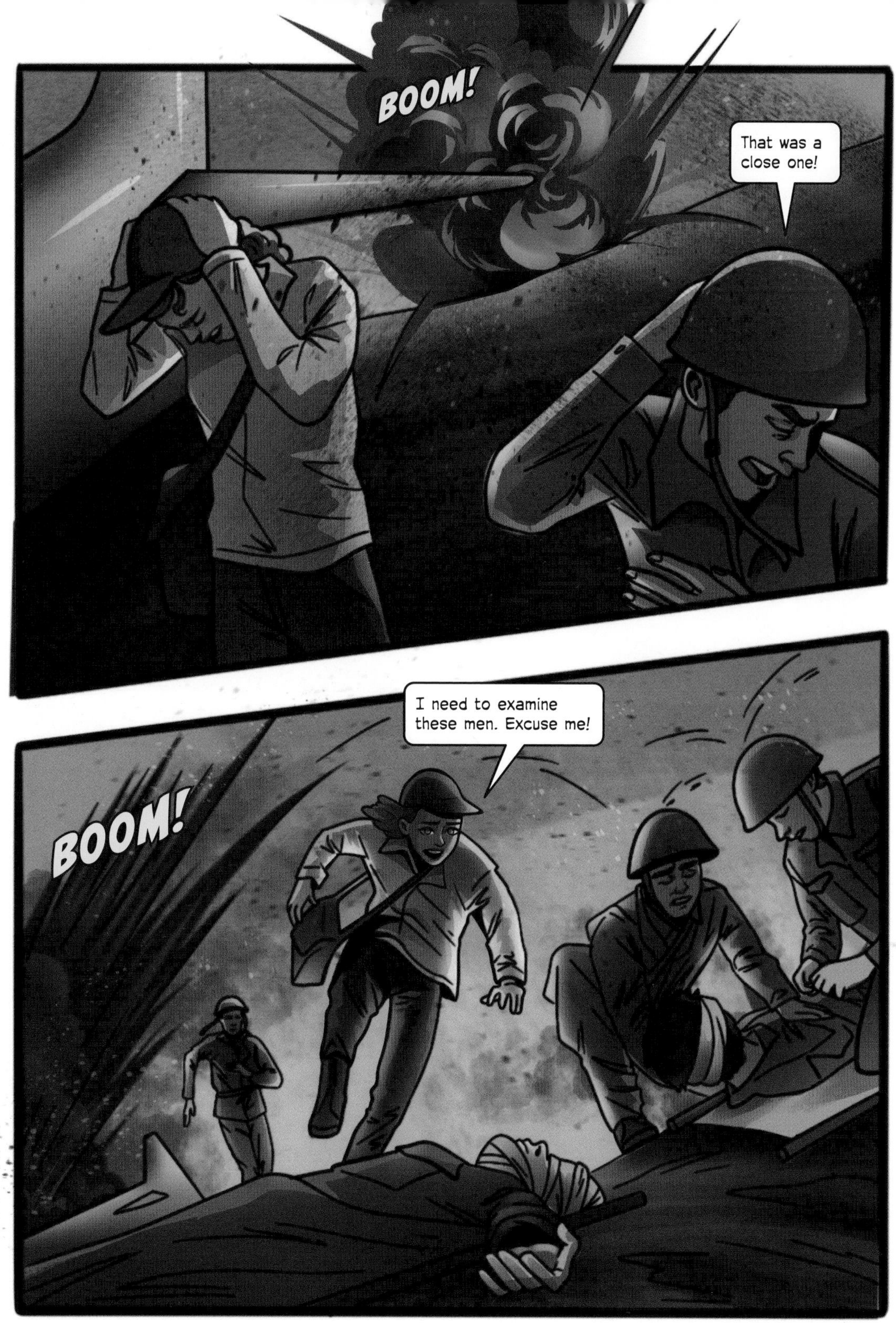
BOOM!
That was a close one!
I need to examine these men. Excuse me!
BOOM!

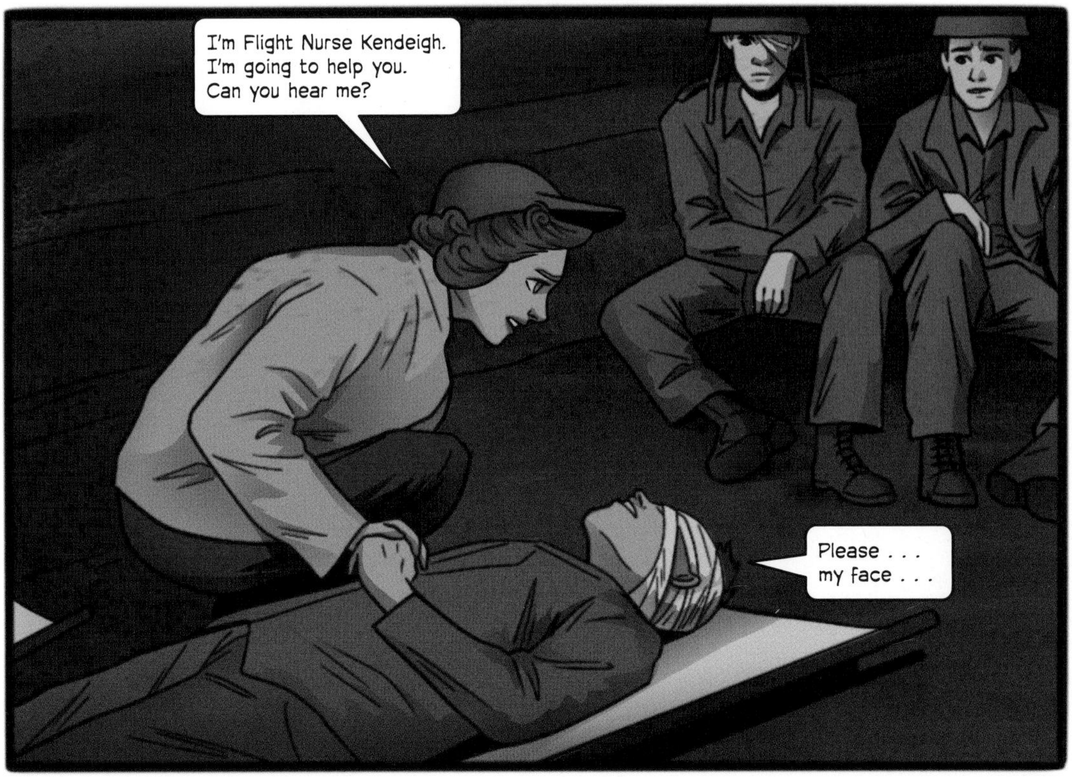
I'm Flight Nurse Kendeigh. I'm going to help you. Can you hear me?
Please . . . my face . . .

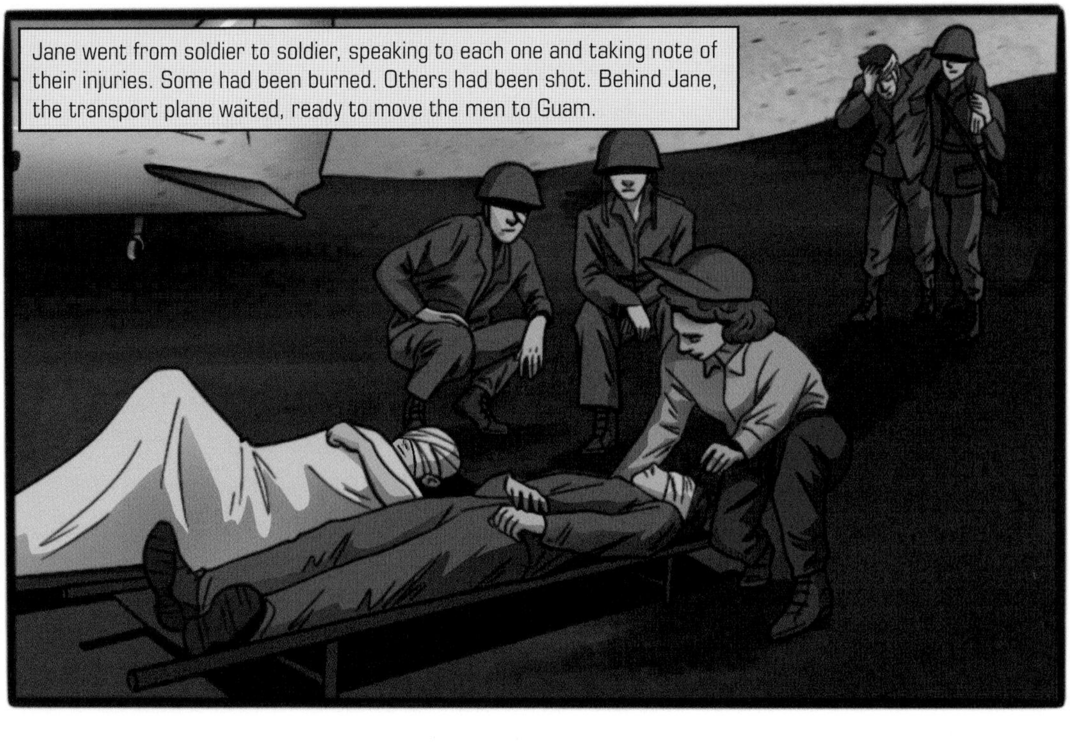
Jane went from soldier to soldier, speaking to each one and taking note of their injuries. Some had been burned. Others had been shot. Behind Jane, the transport plane waited, ready to move the men to Guam.

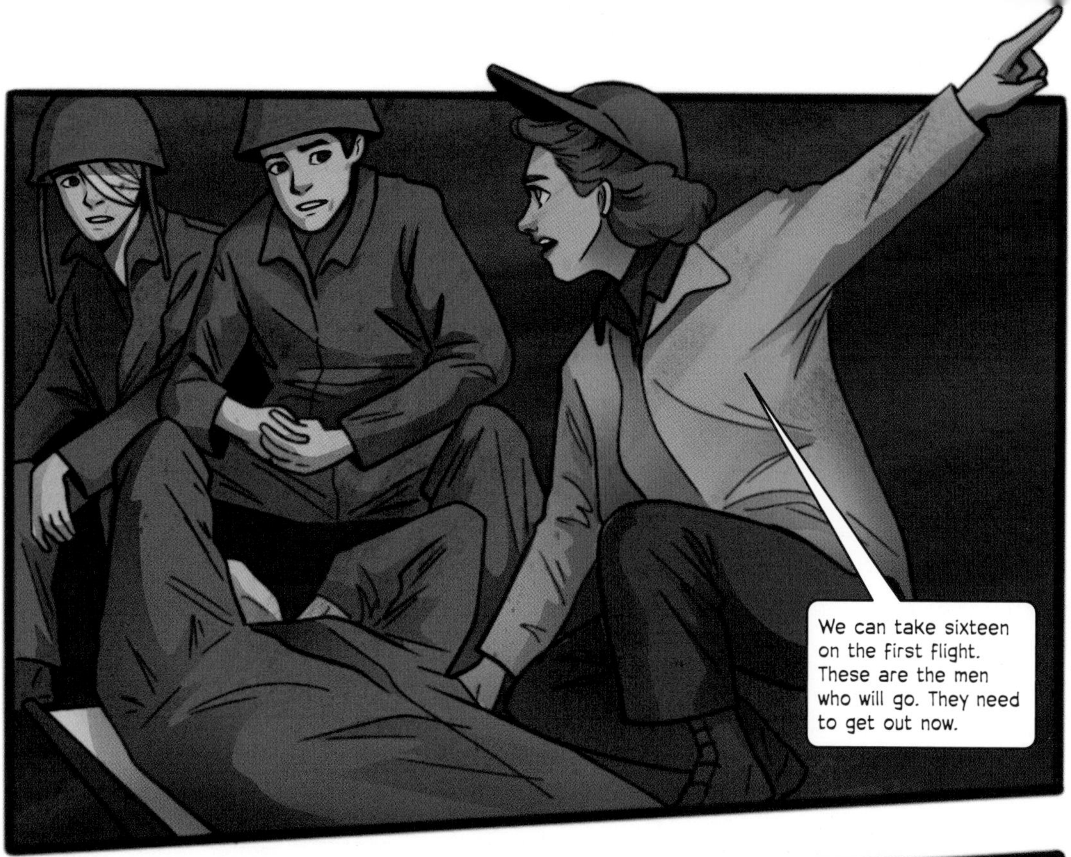
We can take sixteen on the first flight. These are the men who will go. They need to get out now.

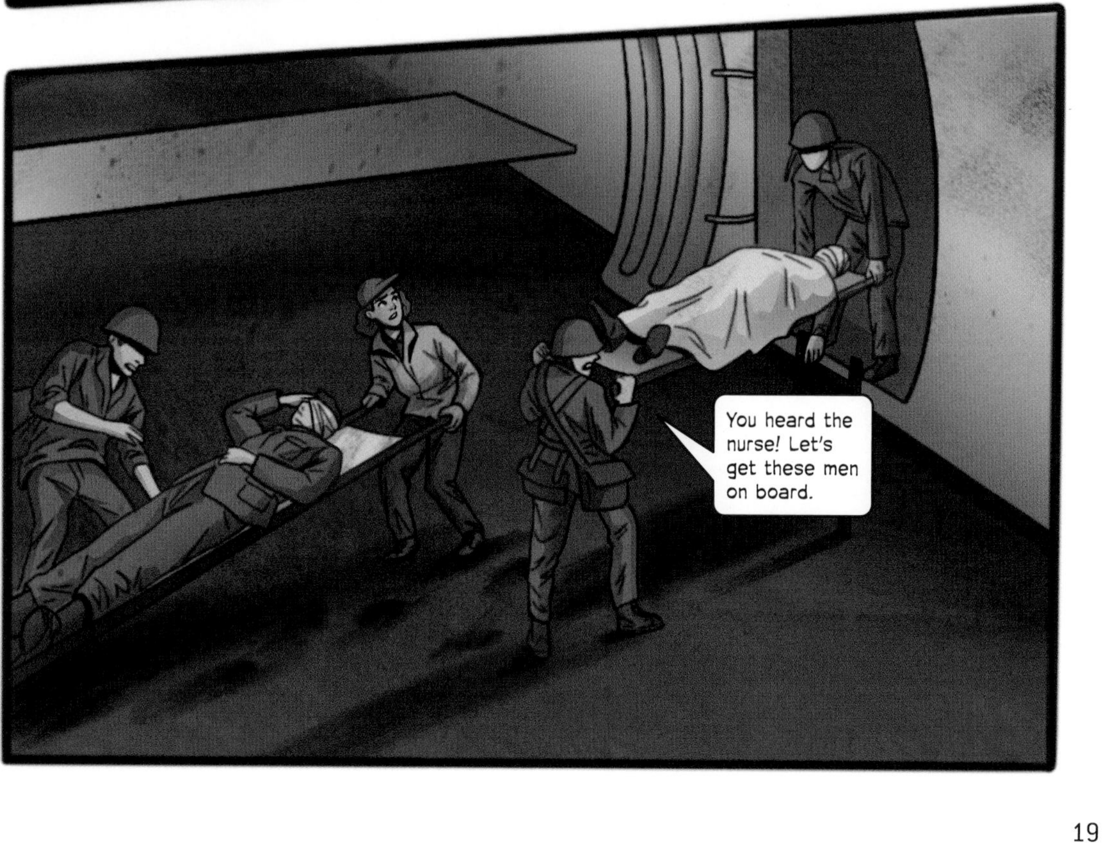
You heard the nurse! Let's get these men on board.

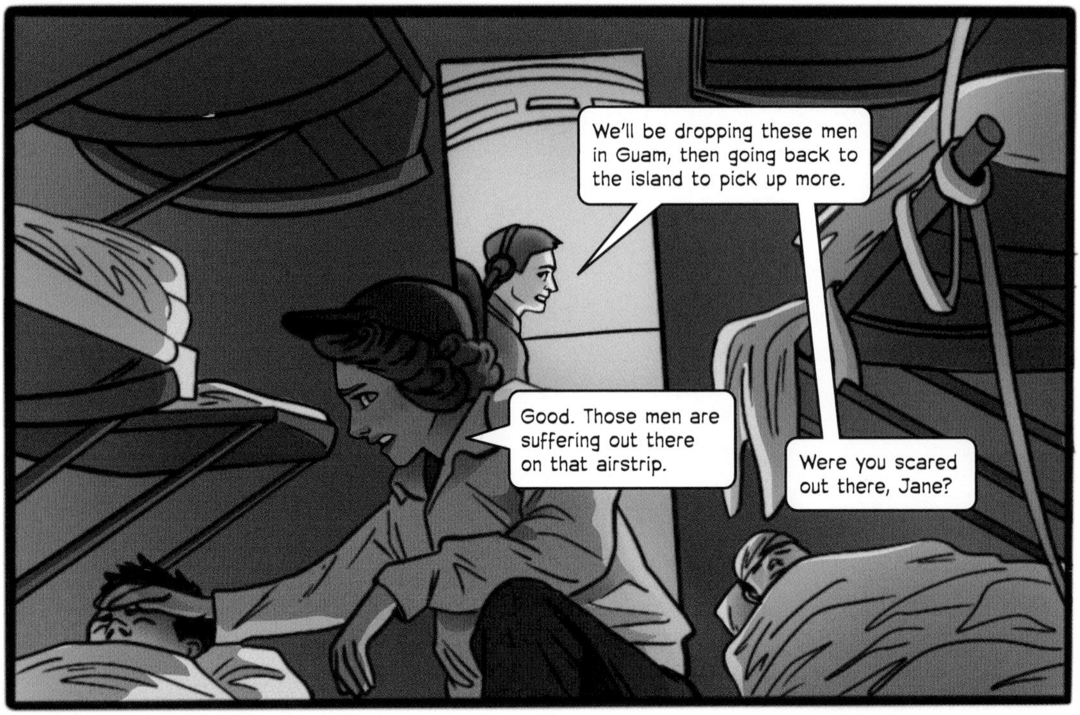
We'll be dropping these men in Guam, then going back to the island to pick up more.
Good. Those men are suffering out there on that airstrip.
Were you scared out there, Jane?

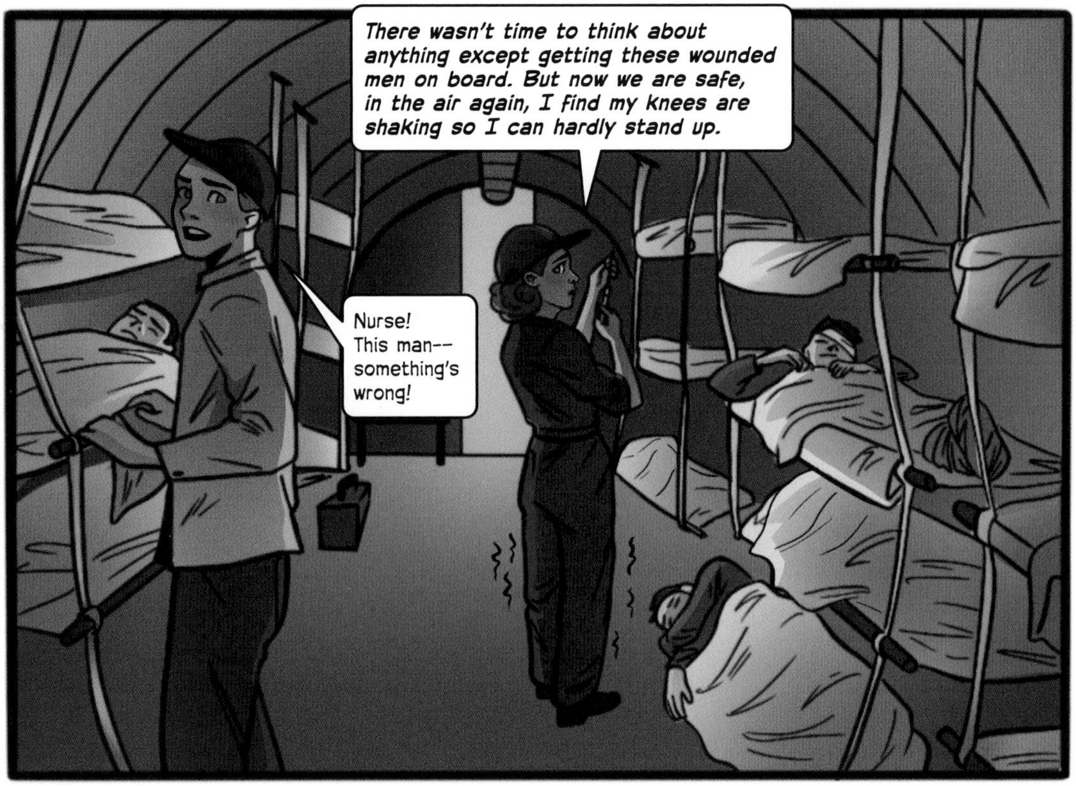
There wasn't time to think about anything except getting these wounded men on board. But now we are safe, in the air again, I find my knees are shaking so I can hardly stand up.
Nurse! This man-- something's wrong!

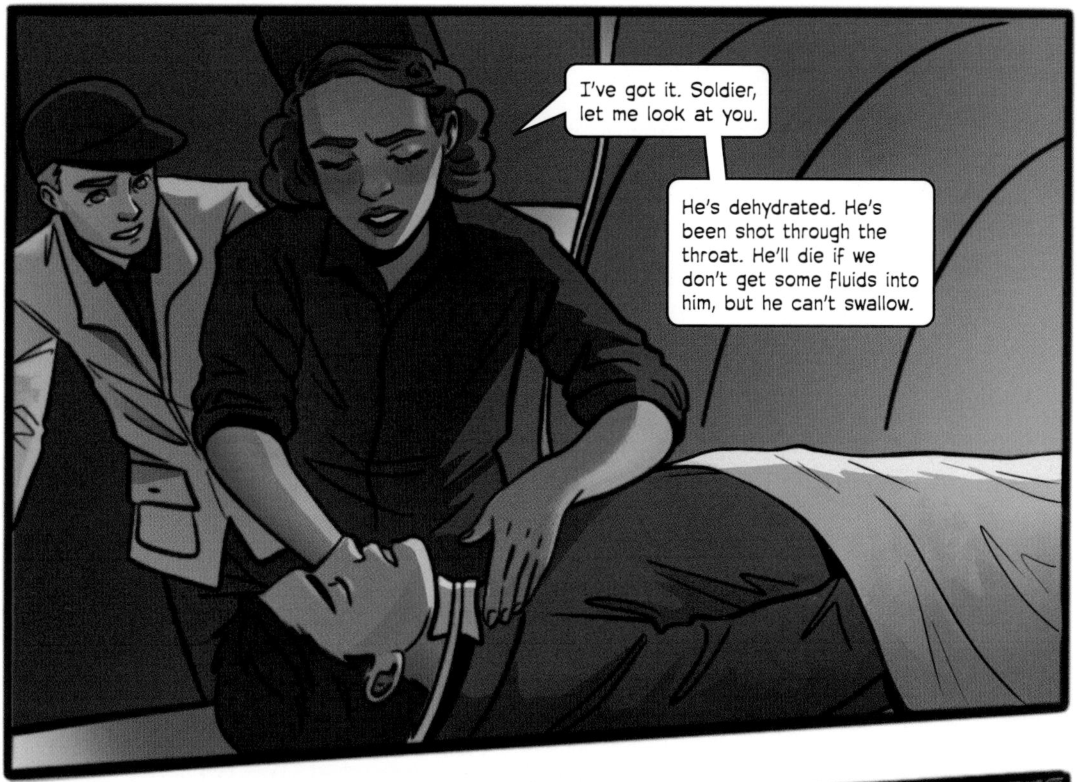
I've got it. Soldier, let me look at you.
He's dehydrated. He's been shot through the throat. He'll die if we don't get some fluids into him, but he can't swallow.

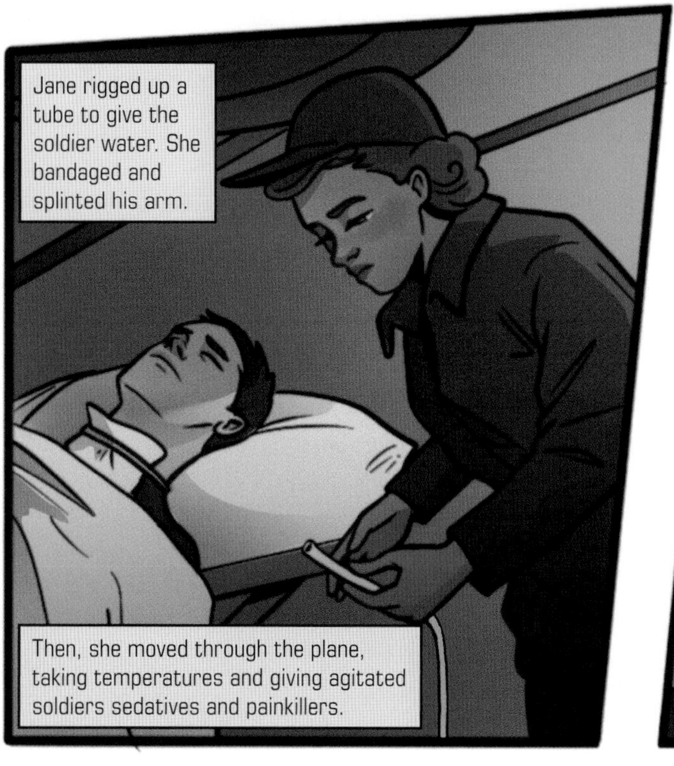
Jane rigged up a tube to give the soldier water. She bandaged and splinted his arm.
Then, she moved through the plane, taking temperatures and giving agitated soldiers sedatives and painkillers.

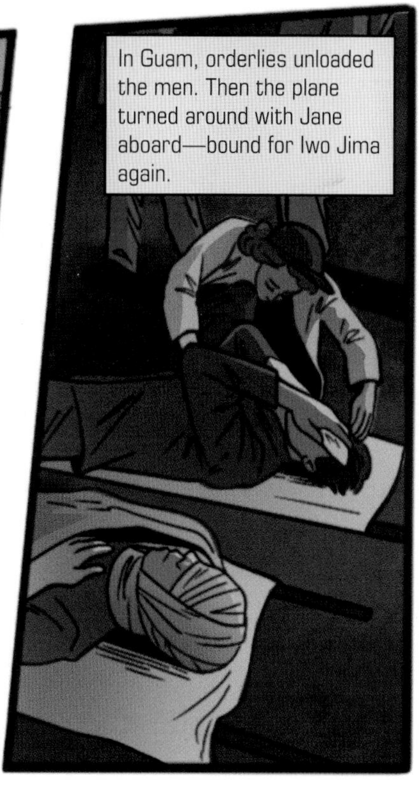
In Guam, orderlies unloaded the men. Then the plane turned around with Jane aboard—bound for Iwo Jima again.

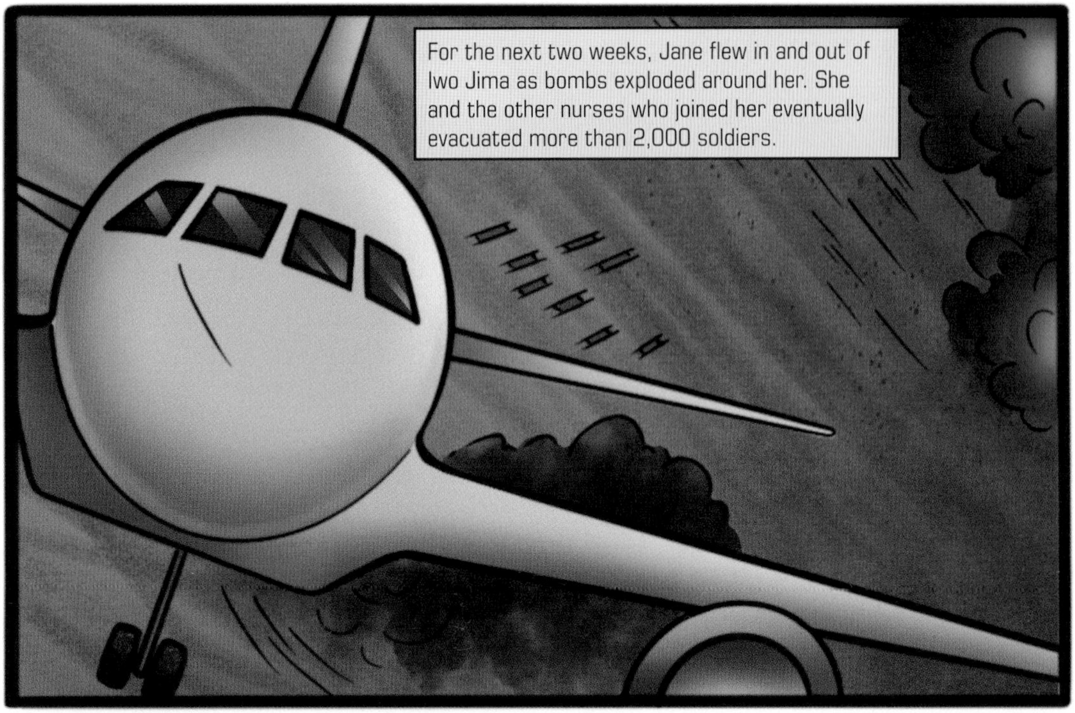
For the next two weeks, Jane flew in and out of Iwo Jima as bombs exploded around her. She and the other nurses who joined her eventually evacuated more than 2,000 soldiers.

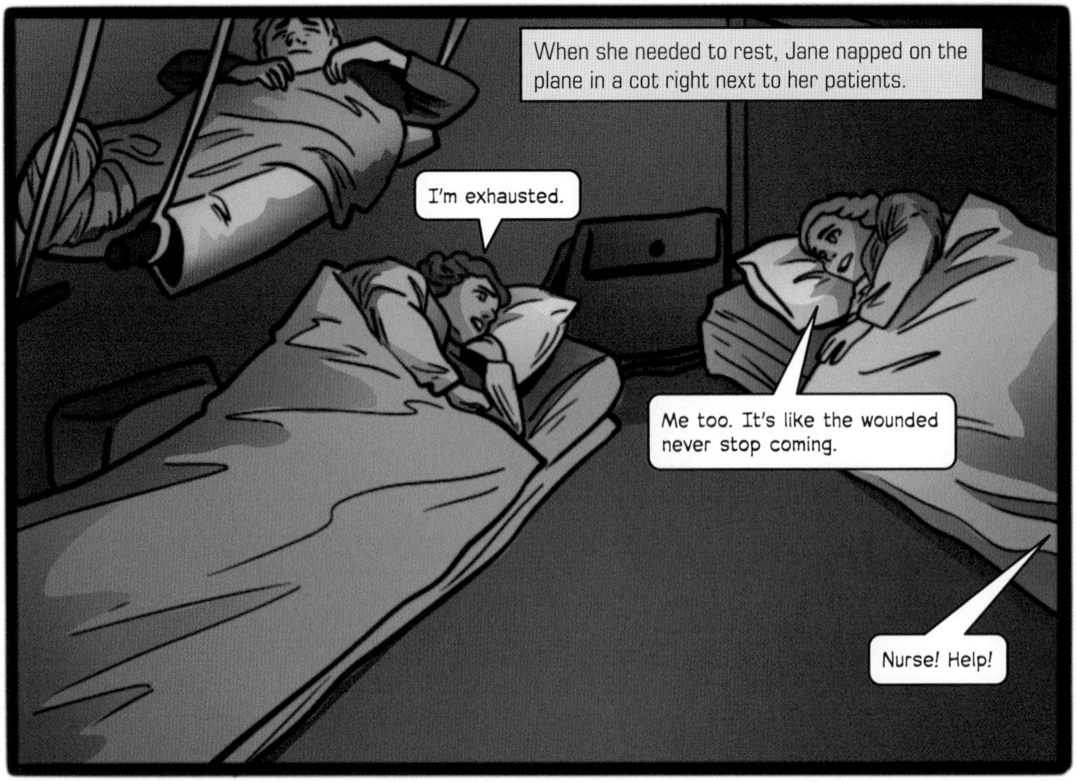
When she needed to rest, Jane napped on the plane in a cot right next to her patients.
I'm exhausted.
Me too. It's like the wounded never stop coming.
Nurse! Help!

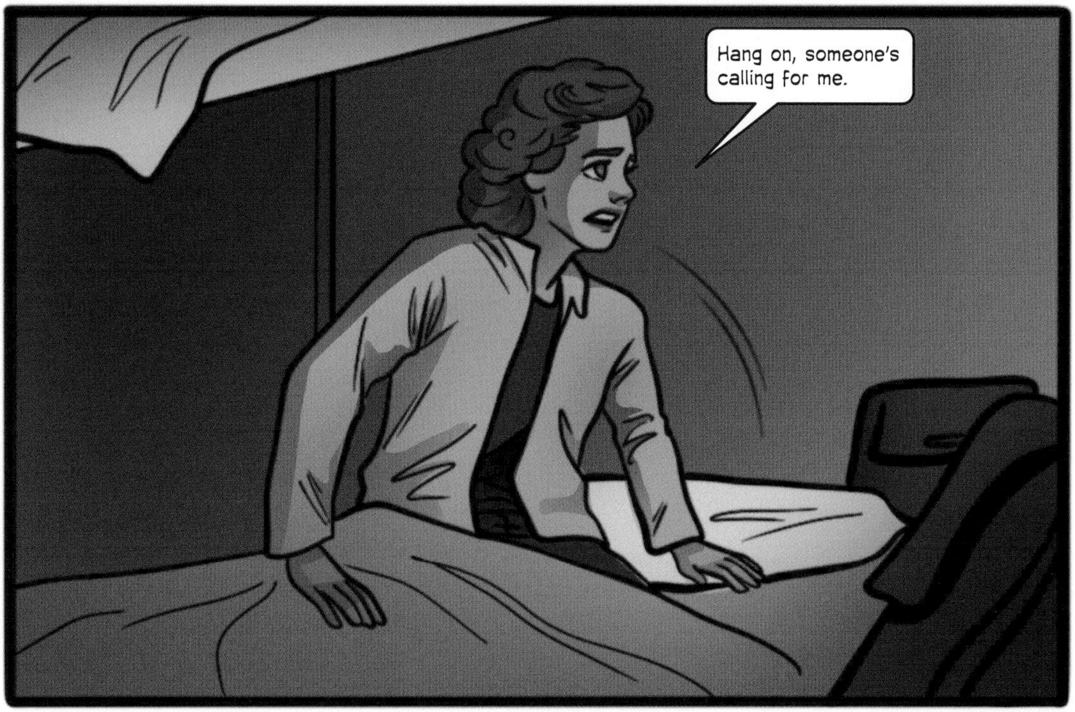
Hang on, someone's calling for me.

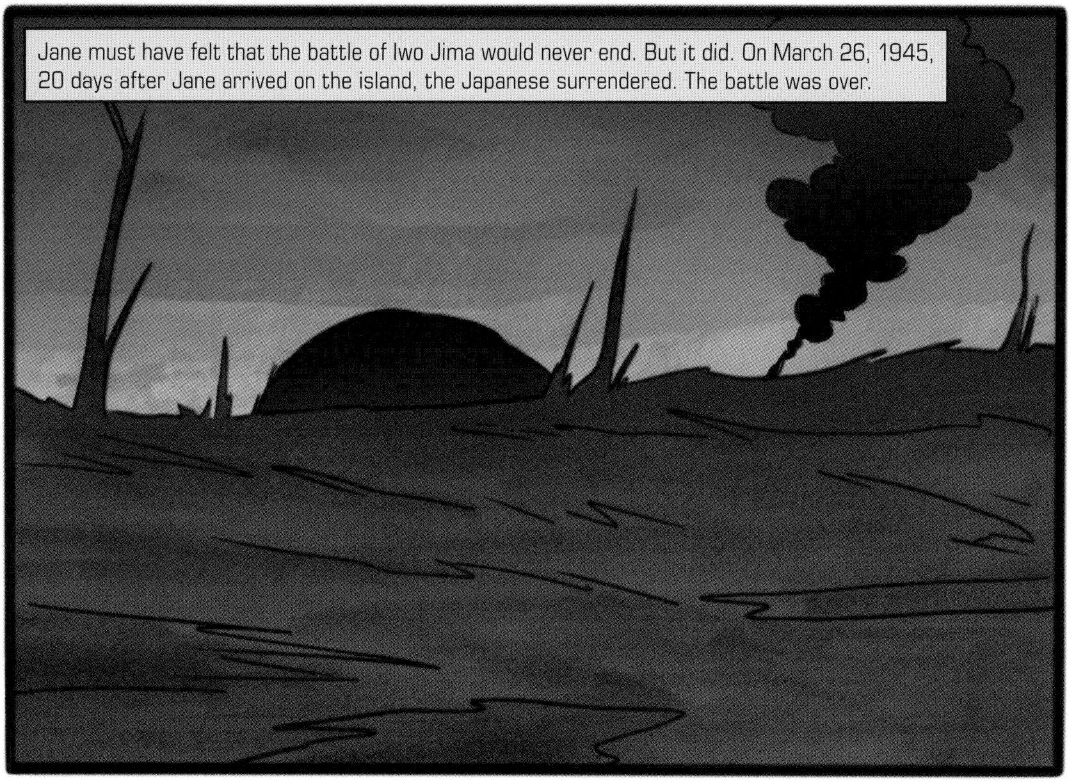
Jane must have felt that the battle of Iwo Jima would never end. But it did. On March 26, 1945, 20 days after Jane arrived on the island, the Japanese surrendered. The battle was over.

AFTER IWO JIMA

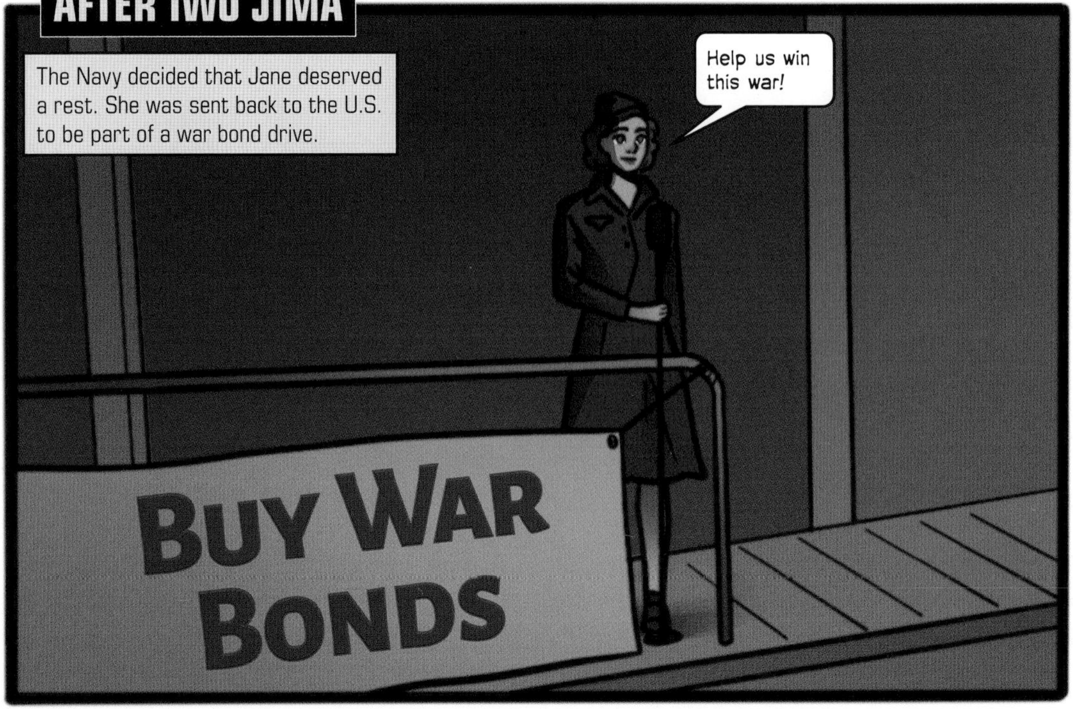
The Navy decided that Jane deserved a rest. She was sent back to the U.S. to be part of a war bond drive.
Help us win this war!
BUY WAR BONDS

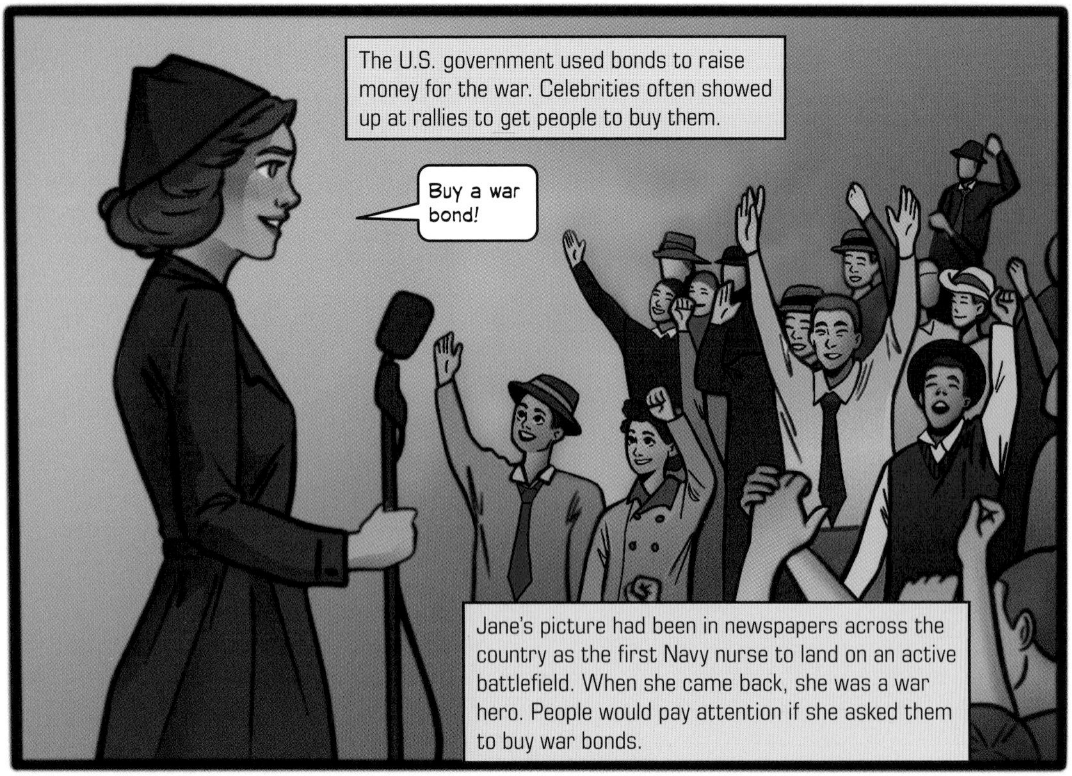
The U.S. government used bonds to raise money for the war. Celebrities often showed up at rallies to get people to buy them.
Buy a war bond!
Jane's picture had been in newspapers across the country as the first Navy nurse to land on an active battlefield. When she came back, she was a war hero. People would pay attention if she asked them to buy war bonds.

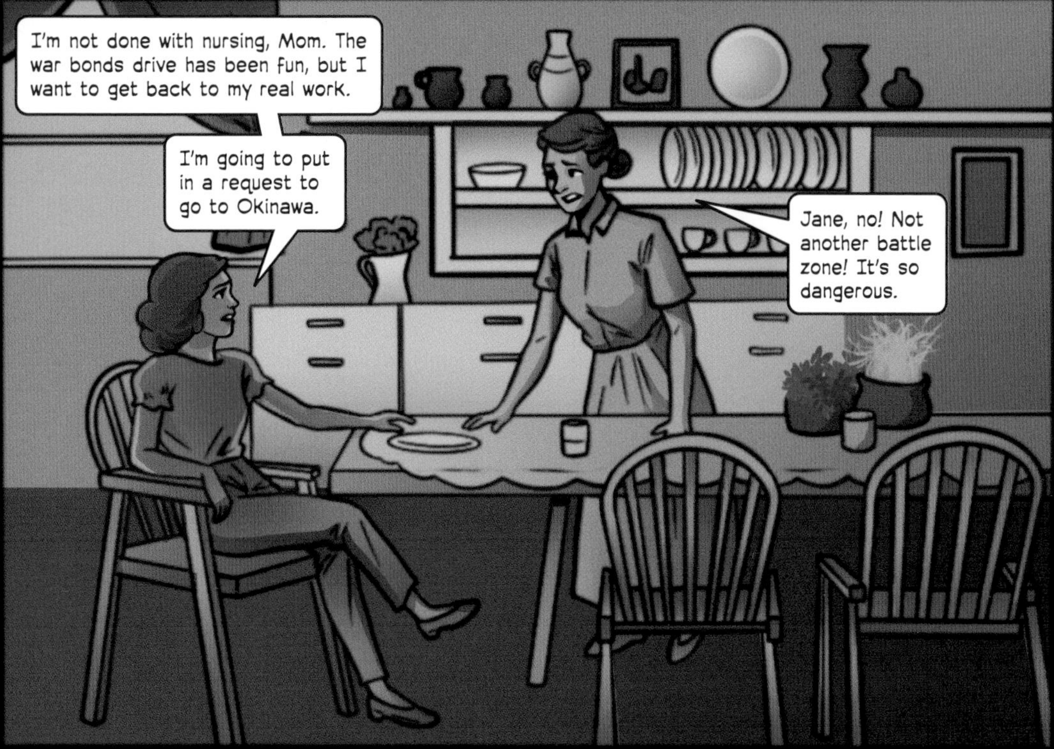
I'm not done with nursing, Mom. The war bonds drive has been fun, but I want to get back to my real work.
I'm going to put in a request to go to Okinawa.
Jane, no! Not another battle zone! It's so dangerous.

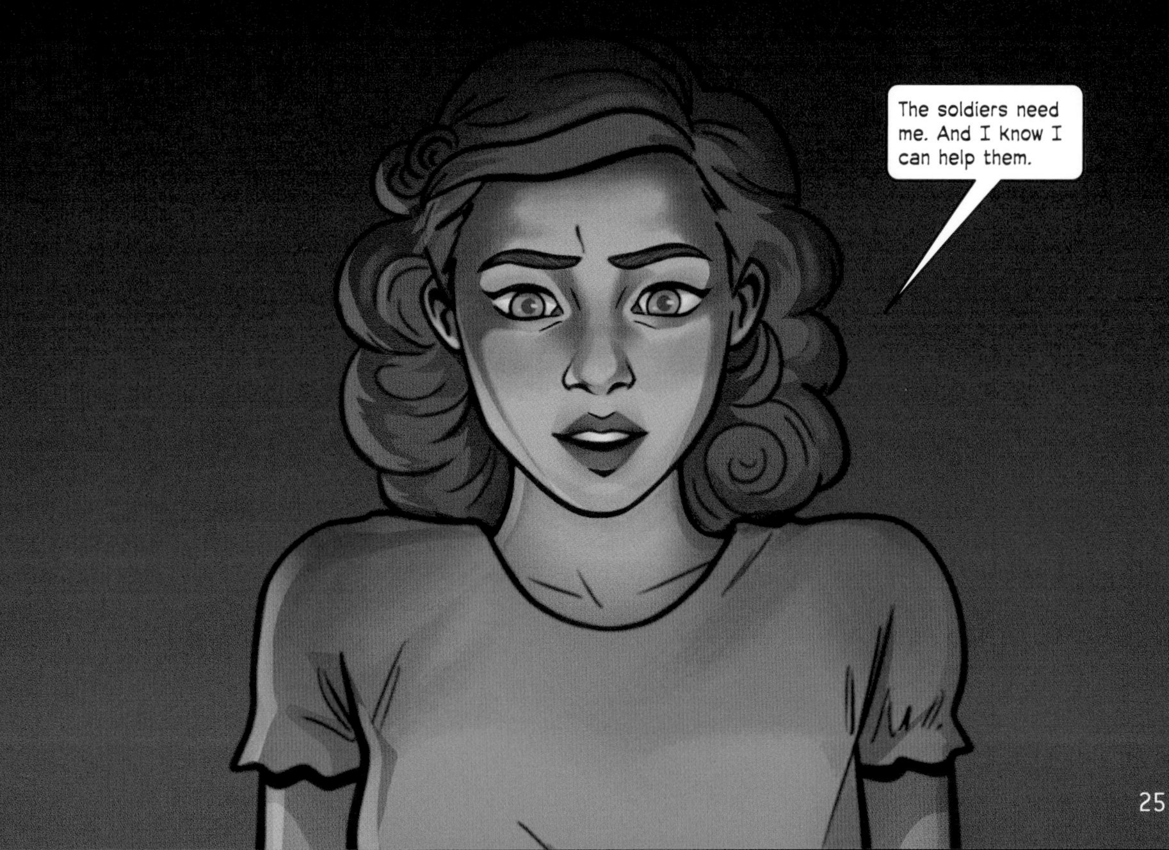
The soldiers need me. And I know I can help them.

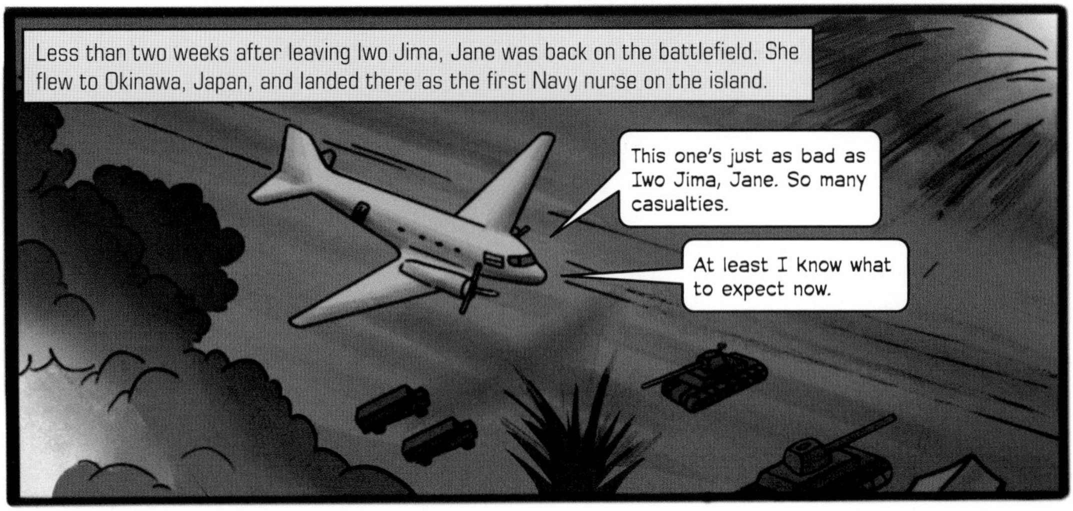
Less than two weeks after leaving Iwo Jima, Jane was back on the battlefield. She flew to Okinawa, Japan, and landed there as the first Navy nurse on the island.
This one's just as bad as Iwo Jima, Jane. So many casualties.
At least I know what to expect now.

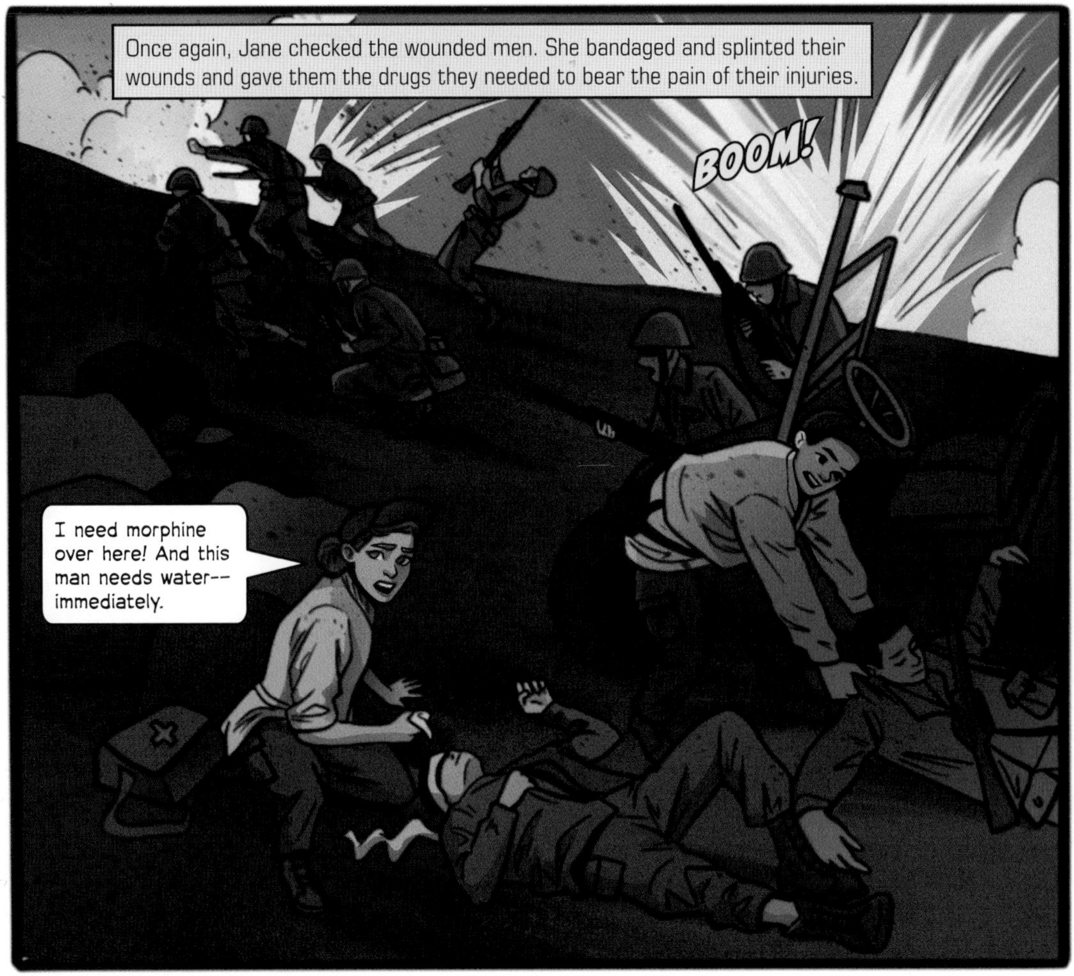
Once again, Jane checked the wounded men. She bandaged and splinted their wounds and gave them the drugs they needed to bear the pain of their injuries.
BOOM!
I need morphine over here! And this man needs water--immediately.

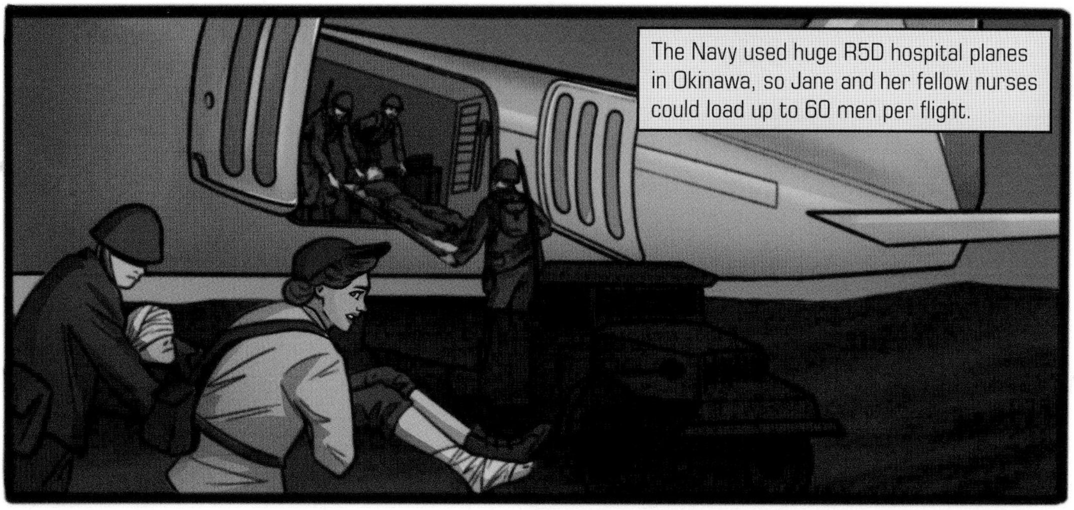
The Navy used huge R5D hospital planes in Okinawa, so Jane and her fellow nurses could load up to 60 men per flight.

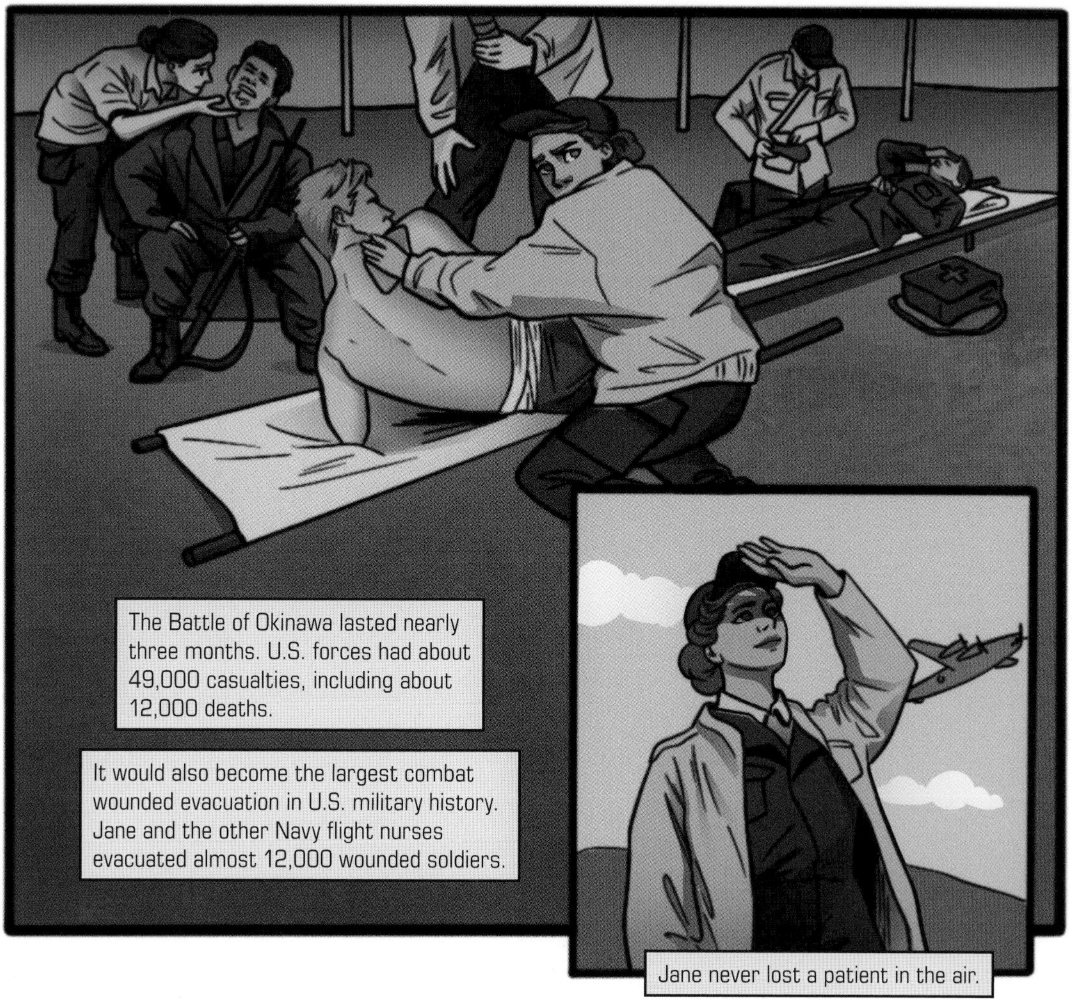
The Battle of Okinawa lasted nearly three months. U.S. forces had about 49,000 casualties, including about 12,000 deaths.
It would also become the largest combat wounded evacuation in U.S. military history. Jane and the other Navy flight nurses evacuated almost 12,000 wounded soldiers.
Jane never lost a patient in the air.

BRAVERY REMEMBERED

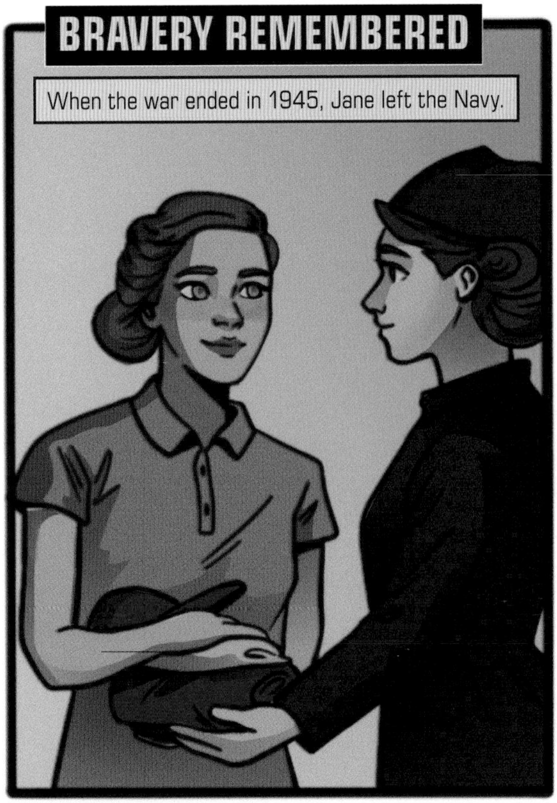
When the war ended in 1945, Jane left the Navy.

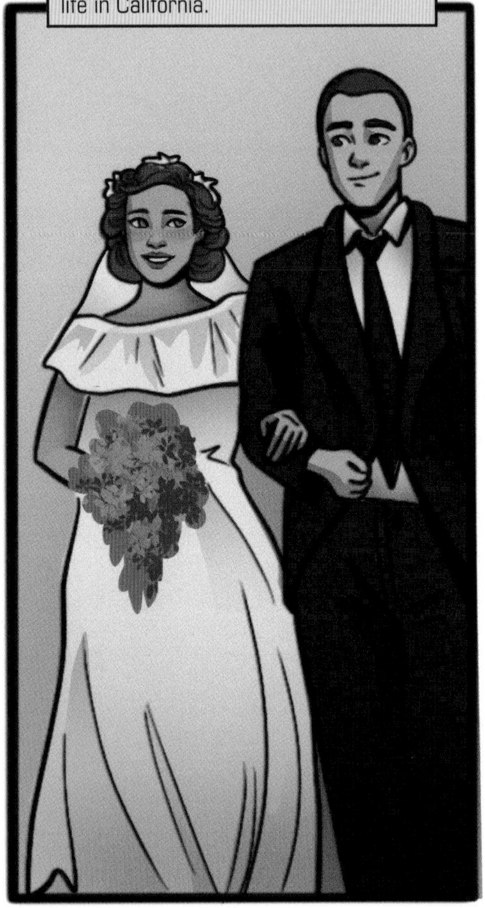
She married a Navy lieutenant, Robert Cheverton, in 1946—a year after Okinawa. Jane and Robert had three daughters. They lived a quiet, happy life in California.

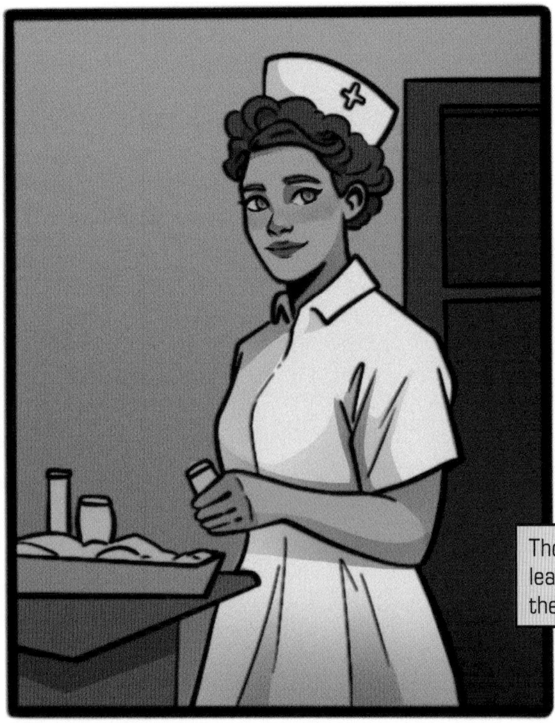
Though Jane had left the Navy, she didn't leave nursing. She remained a nurse for the rest of her working life.

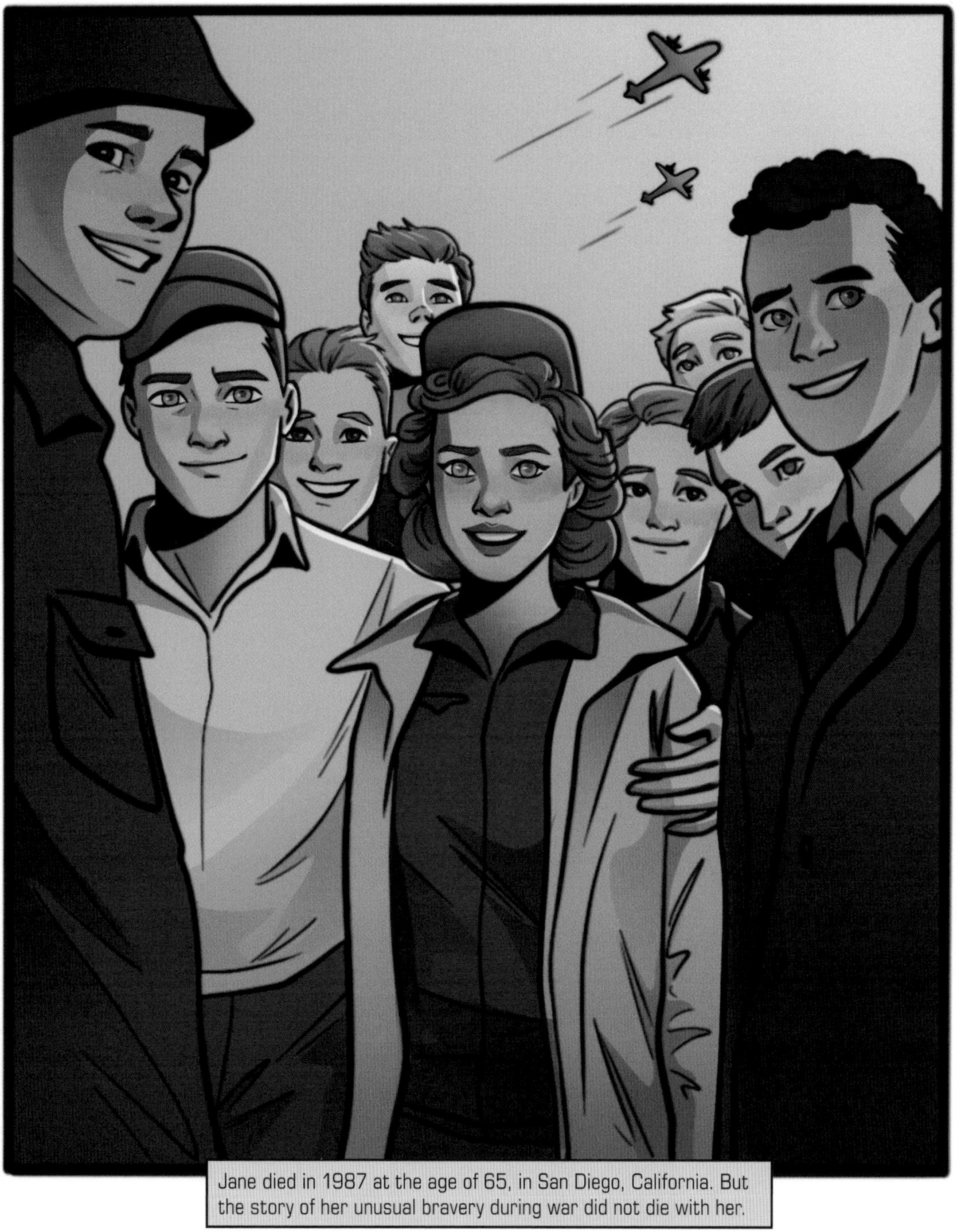

Jane died in 1987 at the age of 65, in San Diego, California. But the story of her unusual bravery during war did not die with her.

Today, Jane is remembered for being the first Navy flight nurse on the ground in Iwo Jima. She showed unflinching courage in the middle of battle. And she used skill and compassion to take care of thousands of soldiers who needed her.

GLOSSARY

agitated (AJ-ih-tay-tid)—upset or disturbed

artillery (ar-TI-luhr-ee)—cannons and other large guns used during battles

craggy (KRAG-ee)—having lots of steep, rugged rocks

mortar (MOR-tur)—a short cannon that fires shells or rockets high in the air; sometimes used to refer to the shells from this weapon

neutral (NOO-truhl)—not taking any side in war

orderly (OR-der-lee)—a soldier who performs various tasks assigned by an officer

rage (RAYJ)—to continue with great intensity

unconscious (uhn-KON-shuhss)—not awake; not able to see, feel, or think

unflinching (uhn-FLIN-ching)—not drawing back or changing

unpressurized (un-PRESH-uhr-ized)—not having a normal level of air pressure

valedictorian (val-i-dik-TOHR-ee-uhn)—the student with the highest academic achievement in a graduating class

READ MORE

Biskup, Agnieszka. *Angels of Bataan and Corregidor: The Heroic Nurses of World War II*. North Mankato, MN: Capstone Press, 2023.

Gunderson, Jessica. *Nancy Wake: Fearless Spy of World War II*. North Mankato, MN: Capstone Press, 2023.

Taylor, Susan. *Women in World War Two*. New York: Children's Press, 2021.

INTERNET SITES

DK Find Out!: World War II
dkfindout.com/us/history/world-war-ii

National Geographic Kids: 10 Facts About World War 2
natgeokids.com/uk/discover/history/general-history/world-war-two

National World War II Museum: History at a Glance: Women in World War II
nationalww2museum.org/students-teachers/student-resources/research-starters/women-wwii

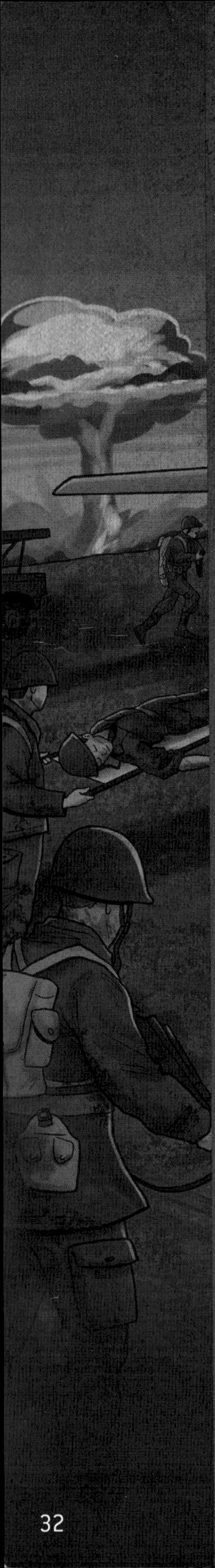

ABOUT THE AUTHOR

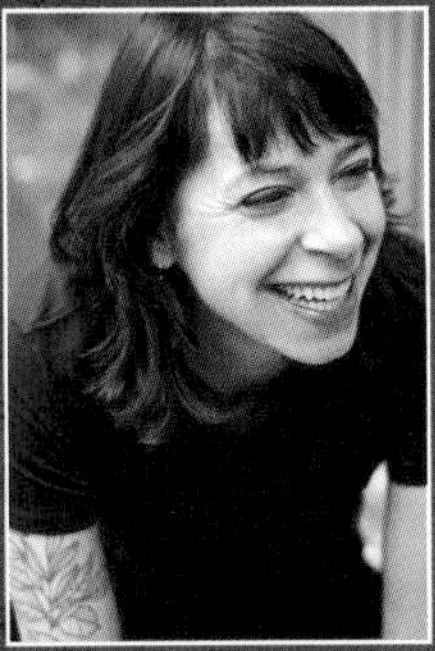

photo by Amanda Sheehan

Emma Carlson Berne is the author of many books for children and young adults, including the middle-grade historical novel *Ruth and the Night of Broken Glass* (Stone Arch Books, 2019), and the historical picture book *Books by Horseback* (Little Bee Books, 2021). Emma lives in Cincinnati, Ohio, with her family.

ABOUT THE ILLUSTRATOR

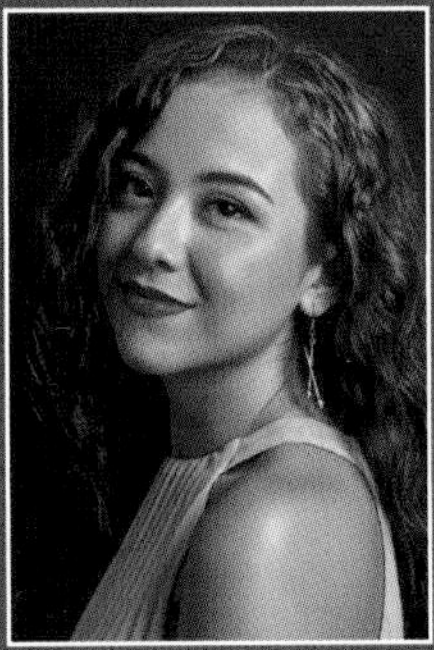

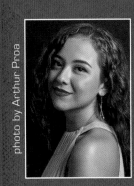

photo by Arthur Proa

Karen De La Vega is a Mexican digital illustrator. As a child, she was punished for imagining characters and drawing during class. As an illustrator, she always seeks to convey meaningful stories and aesthetics through her art. Karen is passionate about books, mental health, cinema, nature, and diverse cultures. She has a degree in psychology. Karen believes that women can become whatever they aspire to be and has proven that to herself.